The Scent of Orange Blossoms

Sephardic Cuisine from Morocco

The Scent of Orange Blossoms

KITTY MORSE AND DANIELLE MAMANE

PHOTOGRAPHY BY OWEN MORSE

TEN SPEED PRESS

BERKELEY / TORONTO

A Kirsty Melville Book

Ten Speed Press
PO Box 7123
Berkeley, California 94707
www.tenspeed.com

Distributed in Australia by Simon and Schuster Australia, in Canada by Ten Speed Press Canada, in New Zealand by Southern Publishers Group, in South Africa by Real Books, in Southeast Asia by Berkeley Books, and in the United Kingdom and Europe by Airlift Book Company.

Cover and text design by Stefanie Hermsdorf

Library of Congress Cataloging-in-Publication Data
Morse, Kitty.
The scent of orange blossoms : Sephardic cuisine from Morocco / Kitty Morse and Danielle Mamane.
p. cm.
Includes bibliographical references and index.
ISBN 1-58008-269-6
1. Cookery, Sephardic. I. Mamane, Danielle. II. Title.
TX724 .M6614 2001
641.5'676—dc21 2001001843

First printing, 2001
Printed in China

1 2 3 4 5 6 7 8 9 10—05 04 03 02 01

Other Books by Kitty Morse

Couscous: Fresh and Flavorful Contemporary Recipes

Cooking at the Kasbah: Recipes from My Moroccan Kitchen

A Biblical Feast: Foods from the Holy Land

The Vegetarian Table: North Africa

Edible Flowers: A Kitchen Companion with Recipes

365 Ways to Cook Vegetarian

The California Farm Cookbook

Come with Me to the Kasbah: A Cook's Tour of Morocco

To the memory of my great-aunt, Tita,
and my great-grandmother, Maman Darmon.

–Kitty Morse

A mes deux filles, Hélène et Fabienne, pour les aider à se souvenir de nos traditions et à les transmettre un jour à leurs enfants. Puissent-elles un jour raconter notre belle vie dans cette communauté juive de Fès et de ce fait la prolonger.

A mon mari, Jacques, le plus fidèle de mes critiques gastronomiques et le plus indulgent aussi.

–Danielle Mamane

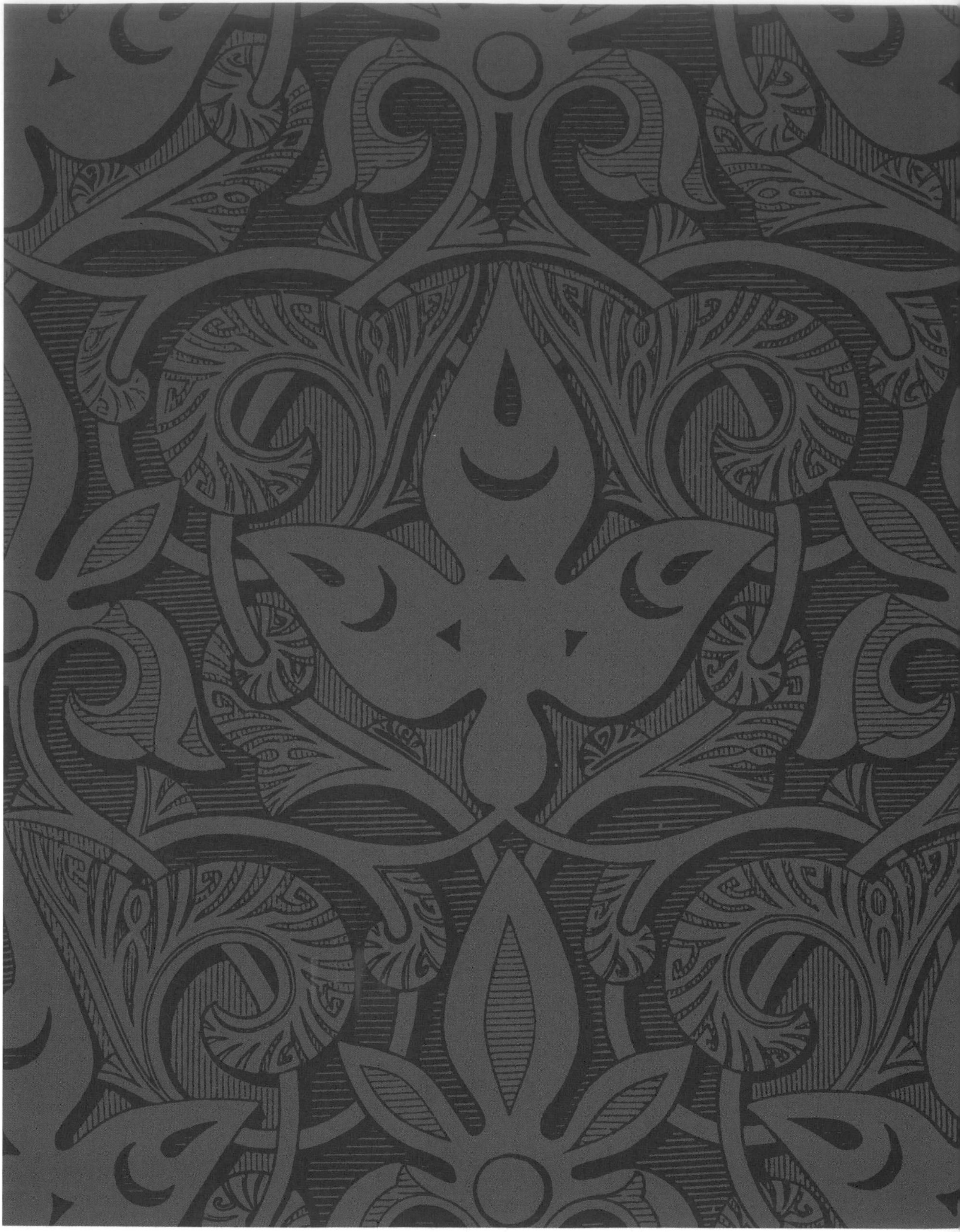

Contents

Acknowledgments xi
Preface xiii
Introduction xv

Basic Ingredients and Methods 1
  Rosh Hashanah 2
Condiments 11
  Kappara and Yom Kippur 24
Appetizers 27
  Sukkoth 33
Soups and Salads 39
  Pesach 49
  La Mimouna 62
Breads 67
  Shavuot 72
Main Courses and Side Dishes 80
  Purim 86
  Hanukkah 104
Desserts and Preserves 141
  Tisha B'Av 144
Beverages 171
  Hillula 173

Sources 176
Bibliography 177
Index 179

Acknowledgments

I would like to acknowledge the assistance of my mother, Nicole Darmon Chandler; my aunt, Martine Darmon Meyer; my cousin, Stephanie Meyer El-Abdellaoui; family members Marisa Benatar and Flor Scémama; Abderrahim Youssi, Ph.D., Professor of Linguistics and Anthropology, Mohammed V University, Rabat, Morocco, who provided linguistic as well as photographic expertise; and my patient and persistent literary agent, Julie Castiglia. A big merci! *to the creative Ten Speed team: publisher Kirsty Melville, senior editor Holly Taines White, and designer Stefanie Hermsdorf.*

This book would not have come about without the support of my dedicated in-house editor, food critic, and now, food photographer: my multi-talented husband, Owen.

–Kitty Morse

I am grateful to Kitty for inviting me to share in this adventure. I have appreciated her good humor and patience during the course of our project. Dear Kitty, thank you for your friendship.

Let me also acknowledge the wonderful women—my two grandmothers, my mother, as well as my mother-in-law—who treated me to delicious food through every stage of my life. In doing so, they awakened in me a taste for la cuisine.

–Danielle Mamane

Preface

anielle Mamane and I first met at her elegant boutique within the legendary Palais Jamaï hotel, located in the millenary city of Fez, Morocco's cultural and culinary capital. My accent must have betrayed my *Pied Noir* (North African) roots, for she asked rhetorically: *"Vous êtes née ici?"* ("You were born here?") And away we went, discovering mutual friends within Morocco's Sephardic community and learning we held the same passion for food, a subject we would discuss at length that very evening around the dinner table at Danielle's villa. There I met her charming, good-natured husband, Jacques, a gregarious, quadrilingual raconteur. Dinner began with the most delightful salad of vine-ripened tomatoes, bits of Moroccan preserved lemon, olive oil, and a hint of red wine vinegar. I knew, as soon as the first spoonful slid onto my tongue, I had found a new soul mate.

Danielle and I began an intercontinental correspondence. The following year, she agreed to prepare a traditional Sephardic luncheon for the members of my annual culinary tour to Morocco. Seven years later, lunch at the Mamanes' tree-shaded villa in Fez-el-Jdid, has become one of the trip's gastronomic highlights.

After each tour, letters soliciting Danielle's recipes appear in my mailbox within days of my return to the United States. The requests have presented a problem since Danielle had no written recipes. Like most Moroccan cooks, she adhered to the culinary philosophy expressed in the Arabic adage, *Eenek me zanek,* ("Let your eyes be your measure"). I sent her a set of standard American measures to help solve our dilemma. She preferred her own *verres à thé, cuillères à soupe,* and *cuillères à café.* The task of conversion into cups, tablespoons, and teaspoons fell to me. This was when the idea of collaboration on a Sephardic cookbook began to germinate.

Barely a dozen families remain in Fez's once thriving Sephardic community. As one of its members, Danielle began to share my sense of urgency at the need to record and preserve recipes that had been handed down in the oral tradition since the time of her forebears' expulsion from *Al Andalus* (Spain). I, too, wanted to celebrate the memory of my own maternal antecedents, who fled the horrors of the Spanish Inquisition and resettled near Oran, Algeria. In the early 1900s, they migrated to Tétouan, a city in northern Morocco steeped in Andalusian tradition.

The fast pace of modern life and the continuing emigration of Morocco's Sephardim to Europe, Israel, and the Americas foreshadows the end of a rich culinary tradition. *The Scent of Orange Blossoms* is our way of honoring and preserving the culture and cuisine of Morocco's Jews.

Tarbah! (Literally: "May you win!") We wish you only the best.

—Kitty Morse

Aflalo and Benzimra families gathered for a wedding celebration, Fez, circa 1940. (Photo courtesy Aflalo-Benzimra family collection.)

Introduction

ike Proust biting into a madeleine and recalling his lost youth, the subtle fragrance of orange blossoms reminds expatriate Moroccan Jews of balmy evenings in Fez or Tétouan, when the heady scent of citrus heralds the onset of spring. They wistfully recall the orange blossom–scented couscous of the last evening of Passover; fragrant mint tea enhanced with freshly picked citrus flowers; and the delicate flavor of orange petals in the ambrosial jam served on Rosh Hashanah. The roots of North Africa's Jews, like those of the orange tree, reach deeply into the soil of the Maghreb.

Some historians believe that ancient Hebrews accompanied the Phoenician traders who first sailed to the northwest African coast a thousand years before the common era. Others theorize that bands of Israelites, fleeing Jerusalem after the first destruction of the temple in the sixth century B.C.E., established settlements in remote oases on the western edge of the Sahara.

The Diaspora that followed the second destruction of the temple in 70 C.E. brought a wave of immigrant Jews to Mauretania Tingitana, as the Romans called their westernmost Mediterranean province, where the topography and climate were similar to those of the land of Canaan.

By the third century C.E., Jewish settlements dotted the Roman province. The indigenous Berbers were sympathetic to the Jewish concept of monotheism. Conversely, Jews assimilated much of Berber culture and tradition into their own lifestyle. They assembled into regional tribes, from the heart of the Atlas Mountains to dusty Saharan oases. They lived in peaceful coexistence with the Berbers, even as large numbers of Jews flowed into North Africa from Iberia and Arab invaders arrived from the East, spreading their precepts of Islam to *Maghreb-al-Akhsa* (the land where the sun sets).

The greatest wave of Jewish immigrants, however, came in the late fifteenth century, when Spanish inquisitors bore down oppressively on Andalusian

Muslims and Jews, forcing them to convert to Roman Catholicism or face exile. Rather than renounce their faith, thousands of Jews gave up the peaceful *conviviencia* they had enjoyed with Christians and Muslims. Once again, they looked to the shores of North Africa. Refugees settled in districts called *mellahs,* from the Arabic *mel'ha* (salt), within the cities of Azemmour, Fez, Marrakech, Mazagan (El Jadida), Mogador (Essaouira), Salé, Tangier, and Tétouan. Others joined long-established Jewish communities in the Atlas Mountains and beyond.

The Jews living in the northern towns of Tangier and Tétouan maintained close ties with Spain. They spoke a unique dialect called *haketiya,* a colorful blend of archaic Spanish, Moroccan Arabic, and Hebrew.

Tammu, a weaver, and Miyyer, a mule saddler, the last Sephardic couple to reside among the Berbers of Ait Bouguemaz, in the central High Atlas Mountains, where the Jews had lived for many centuries. Circa 1986. (Photo courtesy Abderrahim Youssi.)

This was not the case in Fez, a city renowned as a center for Arab culture, where a *mellah* had been established in 1276. The Jews of Fez shared an affinity for the same music, literature, and gastronomy as the Muslim inhabitants of the city.

Jewish immigrants from Iberia were known as "Sephardim," a word derived from the biblical Sepharad (Spain) of Obadiah 1:20. The term was once applied solely to the Jews of medieval Spain and Portugal; today it also includes those of southern European and non-European heritage.

The Sephardim brought a number of culinary refinements to North African cuisine. Thanks to them, New World ingredients such as tomatoes, potatoes, and chile peppers entered the diet of the Moroccan Jews. They favored olive oil over butter. In their flaky pastries, perfumed with orange blossom water, one could discern the telltale influence of the Ottoman Empire, whence many Andalusians traced their roots. They were also masters of blending sweet and savory, today a distinctive characteristic of Moroccan cuisine. They introduced Moroccan palates to the gustatory and aromatic delights of saffron, cinnamon, nutmeg, and mace, whose seductive scents permeate the Shabbat stew called *dafina,* the eggplant *baraniya* of Yom Kippur, as well as the judiciously seasoned *temrika.*

Some experts believe the cooks of *Al Andalus* may have been the first to develop the method for steaming couscous, although others give credit to North Africa's indigenous Berbers for this achievement. Whether Andalusian or Berber, the semolina product remains the staple of the Moroccan diet.

British tea traders established commercial ties with Sephardic merchants from Mogador in the mid–nineteenth century and popularized the use of green tea, which was steeped with mint leaves and sugar to make mint tea. Today, *atay b'nahna* (mint tea) is the unofficial national beverage of Morocco.

Throughout the centuries, Sephardic housewives followed the rhythm of the weekly Shabbat and the ancient festivals of the Jewish calendar. Their daily schedule revolved around cooking and maintaining the household. They were responsible for upholding kashrut, the dietary laws set forth in the Book of Leviticus (11:2–46) and Deuteronomy (14:3–21), as well as in the Talmud, the compilation of Jewish civil and religious law. Among other precepts, Biblical law prohibited the consumption of meat from any animal that did not chew its cud and possessed a cloven hoof. This included pig, rabbit, and camel, among others. Shellfish, and all other fish without scales, were also proscribed. In addition, Deuteronomy 14:21

forbade the combination of meat with dairy: "Thou shalt not seethe [boil] a kid in its mother's milk." It was the woman's responsibility to see that these rules were followed and to transmit them, as well as other culinary traditions, to her daughters.

Shabbat preparations began on Thursday. Housewives formulated menus based upon tradition and seasonal availability of ingredients. In the summer, the unmistakable aroma of peppers grilling over charcoal braziers permeated the Fez *mellah*. Thursday was the day for assembling the infinite variety of salads that accompanied the Shabbat meal—the sweet tomato-pepper relish known as *frita*, mild chiles smothered in pungent olive oil, crimson roasted peppers redolent of fried garlic, and fiery green chiles with preserved lemon. Fridays were dedicated to housecleaning, kneading the dough for the Shabbat bread, and preparing the *dafina* for evening delivery to the public oven. Only after these tasks were accomplished could a woman join her friends for an evening of relaxation at the neighborhood *hammam* (public bath). On Shabbat, she enjoyed a well-deserved day of rest.

Morocco's Sephardic cooks follow the maxim, "First, you eat with your eyes." This appeal to the visual is exemplified in the *jnanat* (gardens), a small armada of seasonal salads named for the lush truck farms that once encircled the city of Fez; in a steaming mound of couscous crowned with intricate cinnamon designs; and in the elaborate array of desserts and confections that anchor the festive table on the High Holy Days of Rosh Hashanah, Yom Kippur, Pesach (Passover), Sukkoth, and Shavuot. A sumptuously laden table is an expression of the love and respect a Moroccan hostess holds for her guests.

Many expatriate Moroccan Sephardim espouse the language and culture of their adopted countries. Yet most retain a visceral attachment to the cuisine of their ancestors. They continue to follow ancient Hebrew tradition by celebrating life's salient events with a communal meal. At the dawn of the twenty-first century, historic dishes like *dafina* and *baraniya* provide spiritual continuity and perpetuate the time-honored flavors of Morocco's Sephardic cuisine.

Basic Ingredients and Methods

Almond Paste 4

Beef Stock 4

Chicken Stock 5

Couscous 5

Olives 6

Olive Oil 6

Orange Blossom Water 6

Peeling Fresh Fava Beans 7

Peeling and Seeding Tomatoes 7

Roasting Peppers 7

Saffron 7

Soaking Dried Beans 8

Toasting Nuts 8

Toasting Sesame Seeds and Aniseeds 8

Rosh Hashanah

In early fall, at the height of the autumn harvest, the sound of the shofar (ram's horn), symbolic of Abraham's sacrifice, heralds the beginning of the two-day New Year celebration of Rosh Hashanah (head of the year), when God selects those for reinstatement in the book of life for the coming year.

For this celebration, housewives bring out their finest linen and tableware. There is a crystal decanter of wine for kiddush. Two loaves of bread and a saucer of salt, one of life's essential ingredients, lie hidden under a delicately embroidered napkin. On this night, pieces of bread, used for the motze (blessing), are dipped in sugar rather than salt, as a symbol of hope for the coming year. Celebrants partake of symbolic foods during a series of blessings, called berahoth.

Zahra Aflalo, Danielle's mother, standing in front of a Berber rug wearing the traditional *kessoua al kabira*—green velvet skirt, lace blouse, and gold threaded headdress—during the week of her wedding in Fez, 1944. (Photo courtesy Mamane family collection.)

First Day

Lunch

Assorted fresh or cooked salads
Holiday Potato and Meat Pie (page 28)
Tagine of Lamb with White Truffles (page 111)
Fresh, seasonal fruit
Quince Compote (page 168)
Assorted pastries and Mint Tea (page 172)

Dinner

Assorted fresh or cooked salads
Cornish Hens with Fresh Figs (page 92)
Sweet Roasted Vegetables for Rosh Hashanah (page 117)
Fresh, seasonal fruit
Quince Compote (page 168)
Assorted pastries and Mint Tea (page 172)

Second Day

Lunch

Fish Fillets Fez Style (page 130)
Zahra's Beef with Preserved Kumquats (page 102)
Ground Meat Kebabs (page 109) or
grilled lamb chops
Fresh, seasonal fruit
Quince Compote (page 168)
Assorted pastries and Mint Tea (page 172)

Dinner

Rosh Hashanah Cabbage Soup (page 48)
Meatballs in Cinnamon-Onion Sauce (page 97)
Pomegranate Seeds with Walnuts (page 157)
Quince Compote (page 168)
Assorted pastries and Mint Tea (page 172)

Basic Ingredients and Methods

Almond Paste

This paste, found in many Sephardic pastries and confections, is made of ground almonds and sometimes sugar. It is available in the baking section of many supermarkets. Some bakeries sell almond paste by the pound. To make your own, see page 159. To store almond paste, tightly seal it in plastic wrap to prevent drying, and refrigerate for up to 6 months.

Beef Stock

Makes about 8 cups

10 cups water
3 pounds beef shank meat, on the bone
1 pound beef bones, rinsed under running water
2 onions, peeled and sliced
8 peppercorns
1 (3-inch) stick cinnamon
1 tablespoon salt

In a stockpot or large soup pot, combine the water, beef shank, beef bones, onions, peppercorns, and cinnamon stick. Bring to a rolling boil over medium-high heat. With a slotted spoon, skim off the foam. Decrease the heat to medium-low, cover, and cook until the stock acquires a full flavor, 2½ to 3 hours. Pass through a fine-meshed sieve, capturing the liquid and discarding the solids. Season with the salt. Use immediately or refrigerate for 2 to 3 hours, then skim off the fat.

Chicken Stock

Makes about 8 cups

10 cups water
3½ pounds chicken wings and backs, rinsed under running water
1 leek, white and green parts, sliced
2 stalks celery, sliced
2 carrots, peeled and cut into 1-inch pieces
2 bay leaves
1 (3-inch) stick cinnamon
5 peppercorns
1 tablespoon salt

In a stockpot or large soup pot, combine the water and chicken. Bring to a rolling boil over medium-high heat. With a slotted spoon, skim off the foam. Decrease the heat to medium-low. Add the leek, celery, carrots, bay leaves, cinnamon, and peppercorns. Cover and cook for 2 to 2½ hours. Pass through a fine-meshed sieve, capturing the liquid and discarding the solids. Season with the salt. Use immediately or refrigerate for 2 to 3 hours, then skim off the fat.

Couscous

Couscous is the staple of the Moroccan diet. The word itself refers to the durum wheat semolina product, as well as to the sweet or savory dish in which it is the primary ingredient.

Moroccan housewives prepare couscous by rolling semolina with lightly salted water, using their fingers and palms to form tiny granules. At this point, the couscous is ready for steaming. Once steamed, couscous can be eaten immediately or dried and stored in an airtight container for months, and even years.

Couscous is traditionally steamed in a *couscoussier,* the French word for the special implement consisting of a colander set over a large, pot-bellied soup pot. The seam between the colander and pot is sealed with a strip of cloth dipped in water and flour, forcing the steam to move directly through the couscous. The couscous is cooked, uncovered, until puffs of vapor rise through the granules. This steaming process is sometimes repeated two or three times, until the couscous expands to approximately three times its original size. After the final steaming, the couscous is lightly oiled, moistened with a small amount of liquid from the pot, then fluffed with a fork. A savory couscous is presented on a large platter and topped with meat and vegetables from the stew; a sweet version is generally garnished with dried fruit, nuts, and sugar. Regular and whole wheat couscous are sold in packages or in bulk in large supermarkets and health food stores.

Olives

Green olives, purple olives (the intermediate stage between green and black), and black olives are staples of the Moroccan kitchen. They are served as a snack, added to salads, or used for garnish. Brine-cured green and purple olives are the ones most commonly used for cooking.

Olive Oil

For cooking, use any good quality imported or domestic virgin olive oil. Use extra virgin olive oil in salad dressings.

Orange Blossom Water

Sephardic cooks make frequent use of this fragrant distilled product in pastries, desserts, and beverages. In the United States, orange blossom water is available in large supermarkets, liquor stores, Middle Eastern markets, and specialty foods stores. Orange blossom water is good as long as it remains fragrant.

Peeling Fresh Fava Beans

Shell the bean pods. If the beans are small, young, and tender, they do not need to be peeled. Peeling *is* recommended however, for larger, more mature beans with tougher skins. Bring a saucepan full of water to a boil and prepare a bowl of ice water. Drop the beans into the boiling water and blanch for 30 seconds. Drain and immediately transfer to the ice water. Use your fingernails to slit and peel away the skins.

Peeling and Seeding Tomatoes

Lightly score the base of each tomato. Immerse in boiling water for 30 seconds, then drain. When cool enough to handle, peel off the skin. Cut the tomatoes in half crosswise and gently squeeze to remove the seeds. Use as directed.

Roasting Peppers

Preheat the broiler. Line a baking sheet with aluminum foil. Place the peppers on the prepared baking sheet and broil, turning carefully with tongs, until the skins blister evenly, 10 to 12 minutes. Transfer the peppers to a bowl and seal with plastic wrap. Let cool for 15 to 20 minutes. With your fingers, peel off the charred skin and remove the core and seeds. Drain. Use immediately or freeze for up to a month in a tightly sealed container.

Saffron

Saffron, the world's most expensive spice, is obtained from the hand-harvested stigmas of the *Crocus sativus.* When purchasing saffron, be sure you're getting the real thing. In some ethnic markets, the stamens of the inexpensive safflower are passed off as saffron. I use the term "Spanish saffron" to differentiate from this cheap imitation. Lightly toasting the delicate threads helps release their intense aroma. Place the requisite number in a small skillet over medium-high heat, shaking gently until the threads darken slightly, 1 to 2 minutes. Do not overcook or they will turn bitter. Grind the stigmas with a pinch of salt in a mortar and pestle, or steep them in a little stock, before proceeding with the recipe.

Soaking Dried Beans

Place the dried beans in a bowl of cold water to cover by at least 2 inches and soak overnight. Discard the skins that float to the surface. Drain the beans in a colander, place them on a clean dish towel, and rub them until the remaining skins slough off. Proceed with the recipe. To quick soak, place the beans in a large soup pot with 10 cups of hot water and 2 teaspoons of salt for every 1 pound of beans. Boil for 3 minutes, then remove from the heat. Let the beans stand in the cooking liquid for at least 1 hour. Drain, and proceed with the recipe. The older the beans, the longer they will take to cook.

Toasting Nuts

Preheat the oven to 350°. Place the nuts on a baking sheet and bake for 15 to 20 minutes until fragrant and lightly colored, tossing 2 or 3 times in the process. Let cool. Place the nuts on a clean dish towel and rub until most of the skins slough off.

Toasting Sesame Seeds and Aniseeds

Place the seeds in a nonstick skillet over medium-high heat. Toss occasionally until they turn golden and begin to pop, 1 to 2 minutes.

My darling daughters,

What a good idea to celebrate Rosh Hashanah! It is such an important holiday, the only one that calls for two whole days of feasting. Rosh Hashanah is the time of year when God reregisters us in the book of life.

Since you asked, I'll tell you how we observed Rosh Hashanah in Fez when I was a child. The whole family, along with a number of guests, used to gather at my grandparents', Joseph Aflalo, my dear grandmother, Esther Aflalo-Benzimra. On the first evening, grand-mère set the table with her finest embroidered tablecloth, scintillating silverware, and delicate crystal. A score of Limoges porcelain bowls held the symbolic foods for the berahoth (blessings):

A boiled lamb's head—to remind God of His promise to Abraham.

A slice of apple dipped in honey—for a "sweet" new year.

A salad of cooked Swiss chard—symbolizing the plants that grow close to the ground.

Freshly picked green olives soaked in salted water—symbolizing renewal

Aniseeds or sesame seeds—representing all of Earth's creatures.

Dried figs or fresh dates—for a "sweet" new year.

Pomegranate seeds with orange blossom water—for fertility.

A bowl of granulated sugar or honey—for a bountiful new year.

A platter holding seven sweetened vegetables: garbanzo beans, turnips, carrots, leeks, onions, zucchini, winter squash, all sprinkled with raisins, sugar, and cinnamon—for the berahoth.

We helped ourselves to each one of the vegetables on the platter, eating them only after my grandfather recited the appropriate beraha. Afterwards, he would say the kiddush, the blessing for the wine, and pass around a communal, crystal goblet. He would then break the two golden loaves in front of him into bite-sized pieces, and recite the motze, the blessing for the bread. He dipped the bread in sugar rather than salt, as we usually do for Shabbat, and distributed a piece to each of us.

After the berahoth, we were ready for the main course. Most of the time, we scarcely had room for anything more, satiated as we were from all we had already eaten. The atmosphere around the table was cheerful and carefree. My grandparents glowed, surrounded by their numerous children and grandchildren.

Unfortunately, our family began to drift apart when I reached young adulthood. Parents followed their children to other countries, or other continents. Today, your great-aunt, your father, and I are the only ones who remain in Fez. And although we are separated from you, my darlings, I find solace in the fact that you are spending this Rosh Hashanah around a festive table with your Parisian cousins. Thank you for the lovely cards of good wishes.

Shana Tova!

Your loving mother and father

Condiments

Moroccan Hot Sauce 12

Danielle's Fresh Chile Hot Sauce 13

Salted Green Plums 15

Pickled Vegetables 16

Preserved Kumquats 18

Preserved Lemons 20

Preserved Lemon Relish 21

"Top of the Shop" Spice Blend 23

Moroccan Hot Sauce

(Harissa)

Makes about 1½ cups

panish explorers introduced New World chile peppers to Iberia. The popularity of the exotic capsicums soon spread to other parts of the Mediterranean, including North Africa. Sephardic palates developed a particular fondness for harissa, a blended chile paste condiment. The piquancy of harissa depends upon the variety of chiles you select—guajillo or ancho chiles for a milder flavor; chiltepíns or red cayenne for a little more intense heat. Commercially prepared harissa is available in Middle Eastern or specialty markets.

8 large or 16 small dried chiles
1 red bell pepper, roasted (page 7)
4 cloves garlic, peeled
1 tablespoon freshly squeezed lemon juice
½ cup extra virgin olive oil, plus extra for storage
1 teaspoon salt, or more
1½ teaspoons ground cumin, or more

With a small knife, cut open the chiles, scrape out and discard the seeds, and remove the stems. Chop the chiles into small pieces and transfer to a bowl of warm water. Soak until soft, 25 to 30 minutes. Drain the chiles and pat dry with paper towels.

In a blender or food processor, combine the drained chiles, bell pepper, garlic, lemon juice, oil, salt, and cumin. Process until smooth. Taste and adjust the seasoning if necessary. Transfer to a clean pint jar. Cover with a thin layer of oil. Harissa will keep in the refrigerator for up to 6 months. Serve as a condiment on the side.

Danielle's Fresh Chile Hot Sauce

(Harissa de Danielle)

Makes about 1 cup

anielle serves this harissa with grilled kebabs. Friends find it flavorful enough to savor on its own, by the spoonful. The piquancy of the condiment depends upon the variety of fresh chiles you use, from mild red bell peppers or red Anaheims, to fiery red habaneros. Whenever working with chiles, wear rubber gloves to avoid burning your hands. And don't touch your eyes!

2 pounds red bell peppers or red chiles, seeded, cored, and cut into 2-inch pieces
10 cloves garlic
7 tablespoons extra virgin olive oil
1 teaspoon salt
Juice of 1 lemon
2 teaspoons white wine vinegar

Combine the peppers and garlic in a blender and process until fairly smooth. Transfer to a colander and allow to drain for 1 hour.

Place the pepper mixture in a nonreactive saucepan over medium heat. Cook, stirring, until the liquid evaporates completely, 25 to 30 minutes. Add 5 tablespoons of the oil, the salt, lemon juice, and vinegar. Continue to cook, stirring, until the moisture disappears, 10 to 12 minutes. Remove from the heat and allow to cool. Add the remaining 2 tablespoons oil and stir until a smooth paste forms. Transfer to a glass jar, and let stand overnight at room temperature. Seal and refrigerate; it will keep for up to 2 weeks.

Salted Green Plums

(Prunes au Sel)

Makes about 2 quarts

housands of apple, cherry, and plum trees flourish in the countryside surrounding the city of Fez. A few weeks before harvest, Sephardic housewives obtain green, unripe plums about the size of pigeons' eggs for pickling. Salted plums traditionally accompany an aperitif. Cooks also use them to flavor tagines of lamb or beef.

3 pounds green, unripe plums of any variety
¼ cup kosher salt, or more
4 cups hot water

Using a sharp knife, lightly score each plum several times. Place the fruit in a 2-quart jar. Dissolve the salt in the water and pour over the fruit. Let stand overnight at room temperature.

The following day, seal the jar tightly and refrigerate the plums for 1 week before serving. The fruit should remain firm; discard if the plums turn soft. Serve in a bowl as finger food as you would olives. The plums will keep in the refrigerator for up to 1 month. (Pictured on opposite page, middle.)

Pickled Vegetables

(Variantes)

Makes 2 quarts

ephardic housewives always had jars of variantes (the Pied Noir term for these pickled vegetables) on hand, to serve as a snack or to accompany an impromptu aperitif.

- 18 lemons
- 7 carrots
- 4 fresh artichokes
- 1 small fennel bulb
- 1 small head cauliflower
- ⅓ cup coarse sea salt
- 3 tablespoons extra virgin olive oil

Cut 2 of the lemons into ¼-inch slices.

Squeeze enough of the remaining lemons to make 3½ cups juice. Strain through a very fine-meshed sieve, a yogurt strainer, or a double layer of muslin. Repeat the process if necessary to remove any trace of lemon pulp (and decrease the risk of fermentation). Set aside.

Peel the carrots and cut into ¼-inch slices. You should end up with about 4 cups. Trim the artichokes, removing the leaves and the choke. Cut the artichoke hearts into ¼-inch slices and place in acidulated water (1 tablespoon vinegar or lemon juice to 4 cups cold water) to prevent darkening. Trim the fennel and cut the bulb into ¼-inch slices. You should have about 1 cup. Separate the cauliflower into small florets. You should have about 3 cups.

Place a 2-inch layer of carrots in the bottom of a wide-mouthed 2-quart glass jar. Top with a layer of artichoke hearts, then fennel, then cauliflower. Sprinkle each slice of lemon on both sides with salt. Cover the vegetables with a layer of lemon slices. Repeat the layers in the same order until the jar is full.

In a small bowl, combine 3 cups of the lemon juice with 2 tablespoons salt. Pour into the jar. Cover the jar lightly with a paper towel and let stand overnight at room temperature. Refrigerate the remaining ½ cup lemon juice.

The next day, the vegetables will have settled slightly. Add the reserved ½ cup lemon juice to cover, if necessary, then top with the oil. Seal the jar with plastic wrap, and then the lid. Refrigerate for 3 to 4 days before eating; the vegetables will keep for up to 10 days in the refrigerator. Discard the jar if you see any signs of fermentation. (Pictured on page 14, left.)

Preserved Kumquats

(Kumquats au Vinaigre)

Makes 1 quart

Rather than making sweet preserves, Zahra Aflalo, Danielle's mother, pickles the bright orange marble-sized kumquats in vinegar. Prepare this unique preserve at least two weeks ahead to make Zahra's Beef with Preserved Kumquats (page 102).

1 pound unblemished kumquats, cleaned under running water
Kosher salt
3 unblemished lemons
⅓ cup white distilled vinegar
⅓ cup water

Place a layer of kumquats in the bottom of a clean 1-quart glass jar. Sprinkle with 2 tablespoons salt. Cut the lemons into ¼-inch slices and sprinkle each side with salt. Cover the kumquats with a layer of lemon slices. Continue layering kumquats, salt, and salted lemon slices until the jar is filled. Top with a layer of lemon slices. Add the vinegar and water to cover. Seal tightly. Refrigerate for 2 weeks before using. Rinse under running water before using. Keep refrigerated after opening to help maintain the brilliant color of the fruit. Store in the refrigerator for up to 6 months. (Pictured on opposite page, right.)

Preserved Lemons

(Citrons Confits)

Makes about 1 quart

itrons confits *are the quintessential condiment of the Moroccan kitchen. North African cooks use* limmoon ed deq *(bergamot lemons) to make preserved lemons, as well as tangerine-sized* immoon bussera *(navel lemons). Thin-skinned Meyer lemons, or firm Eurekas, also work well for making the intensely flavored preserve.*

After the salting process, you will be left with rind and pulp—some recipes call for one or the other, some for both. Any unused portion of a lemon can be returned to the jar for future use. *For sources of commercially prepared preserved lemon see page 176.*

6 to 8 unblemished, well-scrubbed lemons
Kosher or sea salt

Dry the lemons and cut a thin slice from the top and the bottom of each. Set 1 lemon on end and make a vertical cut three-quarters of the way through. Turn the lemon upside down and rotate 90 degrees. Make a second vertical cut, crosswise to the first, three-quarters of the way through. Fill each cut with as much salt as it will hold. Place the lemon in the bottom of a 1-quart wide-mouthed jar. Proceed in this manner with the remaining lemons, compressing as many into the jar as possible. Leave overnight at room temperature.

The next day, the rinds will have softened, and you will have space for 1 or 2 additional salted lemons. Over the next few days, continue adding and compressing lemons until the juice rises to the top of the jar, covering the fruit (this will prevent mold from forming). Turn the jar upside down periodically to help disperse the salt. Store in a cool place on the kitchen counter until the rind can easily be pierced with a fork, 3 to 4 weeks. At this point, you can refrigerate the lemons to retain the bright yellow color. Use within 6 months. (Pictured on page 19, left.)

Preserved Lemon Relish

(Condiment aux Citrons Confits)

Makes about 1 cup

he assertive citrons confits *in this condiment superbly enhance roasted meats or kebabs. Prepare the relish a day or two ahead to allow the flavors to meld.*

3 preserved lemons (page 20), rinsed under running water
4 cloves garlic, finely minced
1 tablespoon sweet Hungarian paprika
5 tablespoons white distilled vinegar
¼ cup extra virgin olive oil
10 sprigs parsley, finely chopped (optional)

Finely dice the lemon rind and return the pulp to the jar for future use. In a bowl, combine the rind with the garlic, paprika, vinegar, and oil. Place the mixture in a tightly sealed container and refrigerate for 2 hours. Return to room temperature and sprinkle with parsley before serving. The relish will keep for up to 1 month in a tightly sealed container in the refrigerator.

My dear daughters,

On this eve of Yom Kippur, I remember the unusual turkey couscous my grandmother, Aem, used to prepare each year for the lunch preceding the fast. Her turkey simmered in the q'dra (soup pot) with plenty of seasonal vegetables, a touch of ginger, a pinch of turmeric, and one or two hot chiles. The aromatic steam that escaped from the stock cooked the couscous granules in the keskes (sieve), which fit tightly over the soup pot. When the couscous was ready, Aem instructed her youngest son, your great-uncle Albert, to deliver separate platters of her delicious creation to each of his three older siblings — my mother among them — who all lived a short distance away.

I can still see Albert straining with the weight of the heavy platter mounded with stock-soaked semolina, tender turkey, and vegetables, and lightly dusted with powdered sugar. I always asked for a taste as soon as it arrived, knowing full well my mother would deny my request. She kept the dish warm — and well out of my reach — until my father's arrival.

Your loving mother

"Top of the Shop" Spice Blend

(Ras el Hanout)

Makes about 2½ tablespoons

Ras el hanout *is the Arabic name for a spice blend common to both Muslim and Sephardic cuisines. Translated literally,* ras el hanout *means "top of the shop"—the best blend (and often the most expensive) a spice merchant has to offer. Vendors often include more than two dozen ingredients in their exotic combination. The following recipe incorporates the spices most commonly used in Sephardic cuisine.*

2 teaspoons freshly ground allspice, or 2 teaspoons allspice berries
1 teaspoon freshly ground nutmeg, or 1 whole nutmeg
2 teaspoons ground mace, or 2½ teaspoons blade mace
1 teaspoon ground ginger, or 1 (2-inch) piece dried gingerroot
¼ teaspoon freshly ground black pepper
½ teaspoon salt
½ teaspoon ground cinnamon, or 1 (½-inch) stick cinnamon

Combine all the ground ingredients. Or, if you are using whole spices, place them in a small, nonstick skillet over medium heat. Toast, stirring, until they release their aroma, 3 to 5 minutes. Allow to cool. Grind in a mortar and pestle or a spice grinder until powdered. Sift to remove any fibrous elements. Store at room temperature in a tightly sealed container.

Kappara and Yom Kippur

The ten-day period that separates Rosh Hashanah from Yom Kippur is a time to atone for the sins of the past year before reinstatement in the book of life. Two days before Yom Kippur, many orthodox communities observe Kappara (from the word "kaper," meaning "to pardon" or "to expiate"). One chicken, substituting for the ram of Abraham, is sacrificed for each female member of the household, a rooster for each male member. Most families slaughter an extra chicken, which they donate to the poor.

Yom Kippur, the Day of Atonement, marks a period of fasting and prayers of forgiveness. It begins at sundown and lasts until sunset the following day. The sound of the shofar signals the end of the fast. As one might expect, Moroccan Jews break the fast with dishes in which chicken predominates, in order to make use of the poultry sacrificed on Kappara.

Eve of Yom Kippur

Lunch

Couscous with chicken or turkey

Fresh fruit

Dinner

Chicken noodle soup or Savory Wedding Flan (page 138)

Chicken Fricassee (page 88) or Tagine of Chicken with Eggplant (page 90)

Fresh, seasonal fruit

Assorted pastries and Mint Tea (page 172)

End of the Fast

Mint Tea (page 172) or coffee with Aniseed Biscuits (page 148) or Bread Pudding with Candied Fruit (page 153)

Lentil and Garbanzo Bean Soup (page 46)

Chicken with Onions and Tomatoes (page 87)

Fresh, seasonal fruit

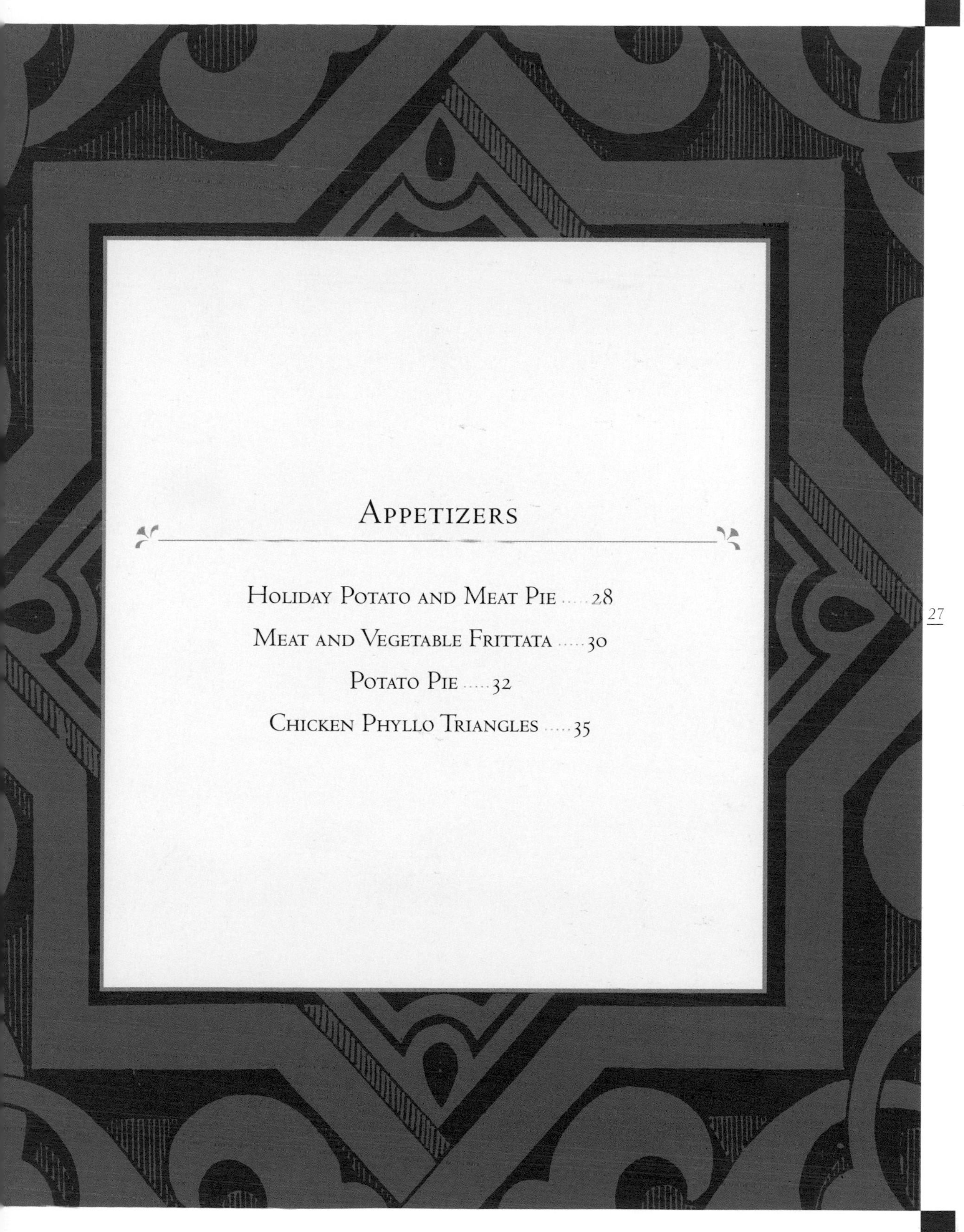

Appetizers

Holiday Potato and Meat Pie 28

Meat and Vegetable Frittata 30

Potato Pie 32

Chicken Phyllo Triangles 35

Holiday Potato and Meat Pie

(Pastela des Jours de Fête)

Serves 12

sing vinegar as a flavoring agent was common in eleventh-century Al Andalus. The practice, no doubt, was a culinary legacy of the ancient Romans. Vinegar adds tartness to the meat filling of this savory potato pie. It is this delectable first course that generally accompanies the colorful armada of cooked or raw salads of Passover.

5 eggs
3 pounds potatoes, quartered
3 teaspoons salt
½ teaspoon freshly ground black pepper
2 small onions, grated
2 tablespoons virgin olive oil
¾ pound lean ground beef
10 sprigs flat-leaf parsley, minced
2 teaspoons "Top of the Shop" Spice Blend (page 23)
¼ cup white distilled vinegar

Place 3 of the eggs in a large saucepan filled with cold water. Bring to a boil and cook for 10 to 12 minutes, until the eggs are hard. Drain and immediately immerse in cold water for 5 to 6 minutes. Remove the shells and cut the eggs into slices ¼ inch thick. Set aside.

In another large saucepan, combine the potatoes, 8 cups water, and 1 teaspoon of the salt. Cover and cook until the potatoes are tender, 20 to 25 minutes. Drain, peel, and place in a large bowl. While the potatoes are still warm, purée with a potato masher or a ricer.

Preheat the oven to 375°.

In a small bowl, lightly beat the remaining 2 eggs. Add to the potatoes along with 1 teaspoon of the salt, the pepper, onions, and 1 tablespoon of the olive oil. Set aside.

Heat the remaining 1 tablespoon olive oil in a large skillet over medium-high heat. Add the beef, parsley, and spice blend. Stir to break up any lumps, and cook until the meat is no longer pink, 8 to 10 minutes. Add the remaining 1 teaspoon salt and the vinegar. Cook, stirring, until most of the liquid evaporates, 4 to 5 minutes. Set aside.

Coat the bottom and the sides of a soufflé dish or nonstick torte pan with vegetable oil. Using a spatula, spread two-thirds of the potato-onion mixture on the bottom and sides of the dish. Spoon in the ground beef mixture and cover with egg slices, reserving a few for garnish. Encase the filling with the rest of the potato-onion mixture.

Bake until golden brown, 50 to 55 minutes. Let stand for 10 to 15 minutes. Run a knife around the sides of the dish and invert carefully onto a serving platter. Slice into 12 equal portions, garnish with the reserved egg slices, and serve.

Meat and Vegetable Frittata

(La Maguina)

Serves 8

he versatile maguina, *generously studded with savory bits of vegetables and meat, is the first course par excellence in northern Morocco. In the following variation, we substitute diced chicken for the cooked veal brains that appear in the traditional recipe. Cubes of* maguina *are frequently served with aperitifs. Sliced* maguina *also makes an unusual and tasty filling for sandwiches.*

4 tablespoons olive oil
1 carrot, peeled and finely diced
1 onion, finely diced
½ red bell pepper, seeded, cored, and finely diced
10 eggs
3 tablespoons unseasoned dried bread crumbs
¾ teaspoon ground turmeric
1 teaspoon salt
¼ teaspoon freshly ground black pepper
¾ teaspoon ground nutmeg
1 cup diced cooked chicken
½ cup chopped flat-leaf parsley
½ cup frozen petite peas, thawed
Wedges of lemon, for serving

Preheat the oven to 400°. Generously oil a 5 by 9-inch nonstick loaf pan.

In a large skillet, heat 3 tablespoons of the oil over medium-high heat. Add the carrot and cook, stirring occasionally, until lightly browned, 5 to 6 minutes. Add the onion and bell pepper and cook, stirring, until lightly browned, 5 to 6 minutes. Remove from the heat.

In a large bowl, whisk together the eggs, bread crumbs, turmeric, salt, pepper, and nutmeg until frothy. Add the vegetables, chicken, parsley, and peas. Pour the mixture into the prepared pan.

Bake until a knife inserted in the center comes out clean, 45 to 50 minutes. Invert the pan onto a rack set over paper towels. Let cool before unmolding. Serve sliced at room temperature with wedges of lemon.

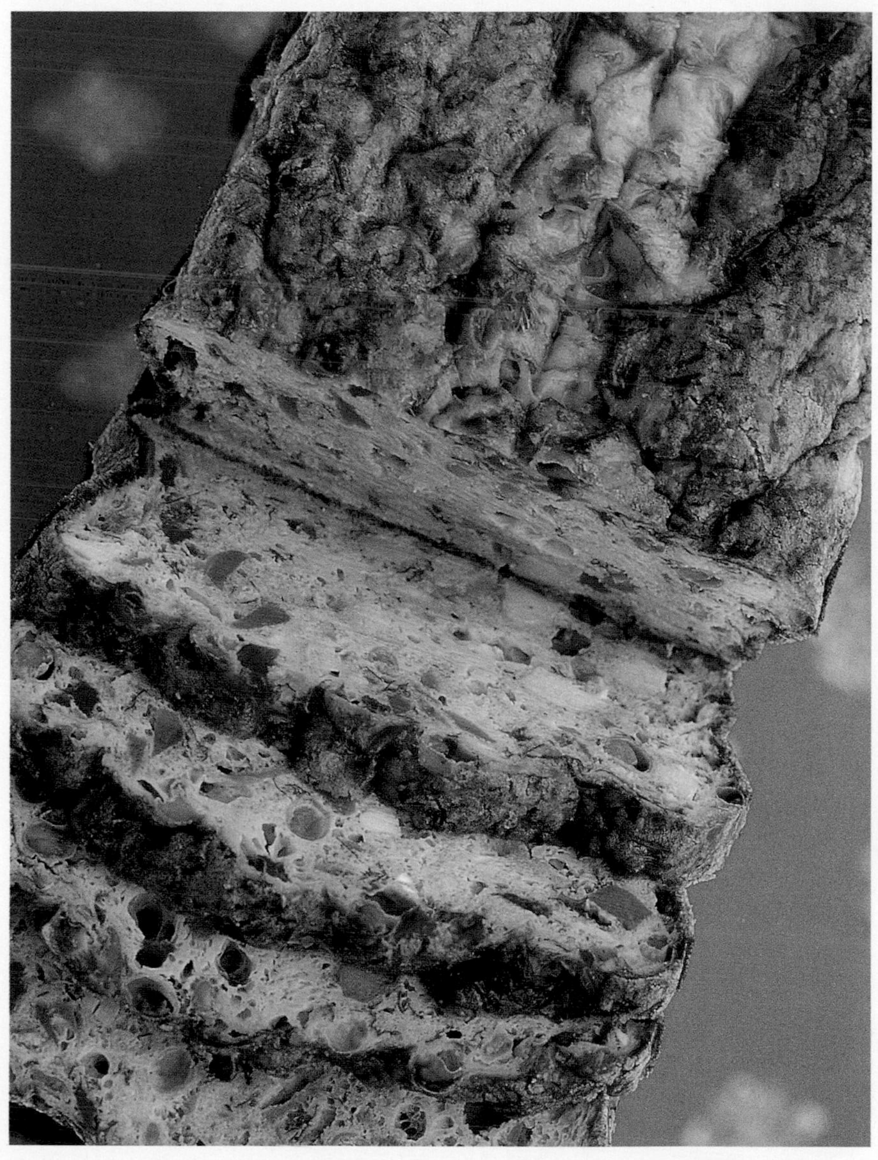

Potato Pie

(Pastela de Pommes de Terre)

Serves 8

his meatless pastela often complements the weekly Shabbat menu. It is traditionally served with Tomato Salad with Preserved Lemons (page 58).

2 pounds potatoes, quartered
2 teaspoons salt
8 eggs, lightly beaten
½ teaspoon freshly ground black pepper
3 cloves garlic, minced
6 sprigs flat-leaf parsley, minced

In a large saucepan, combine the potatoes, 8 cups water, and 1 teaspoon of the salt. Cover and cook until the potatoes are tender, 20 to 25 minutes. Drain, peel, and place in a large bowl. While the potatoes are still warm, purée with a potato masher or a ricer.

Add the eggs, remaining 1 teaspoon salt, pepper, garlic, and parsley to the potatoes.

Preheat the oven to 375°. Generously coat the bottom and the sides of a soufflé dish or nonstick torte pan with vegetable oil. Spoon in the potato mixture.

Bake until golden brown, 50 to 55 minutes. Let stand for 10 to 15 minutes. Run a knife around the sides of the dish and invert carefully on a serving platter. Slice into equal portions and serve hot or warm.

Sukkoth

Sukkoth, the Feast of the Shelters (Feast of the Tabernacles), is a thanksgiving celebration that takes place between the fifteenth and twenty-first days of the Hebrew month of Tishri in the early fall. It commemorates God's divine intervention during the ancient Hebrews' wandering in the wilderness of Sinai. Families re-create small shelters using palm fronds and tree boughs, to symbolize the dwellings that protected their biblical ancestors. Many practicing Jews take their meals and sleep outdoors under their sukkah *(shelter) during this festival. A citron is displayed on the table as a symbol of the earth's bounty.*

Dinner on the 20th of Tishri

Fish Fillets with Garbanzo Beans (page 131)
or Fish Fillets Fez Style (page 130)
Roasted Lamb Shoulder (page 105)
Sautéed green beans
Fresh, seasonal fruit
Assorted pastries and Mint Tea (page 172)

Lunch on the 21st of Tishri

Assorted fresh or cooked salads
Roasted Chicken with Orange Juice (page 83)
Rice
Fresh, seasonal fruit
Assorted pastries and Mint Tea (page 172)

My dear daughters,

Have I ever told you about la visita, a delightful afternoon tea party we used to hold in Fez? Hostesses held a visita to celebrate a birth, a bar mitzvah, or a betrothal. Ladies dressed in their finest kaftans of multicolored brocades and velvet, called kessoua al kabira, and delicate chemises of Valenciennes lace to attend the elegant party, filled with light conversation and music, pastries, and sweets.

My aunt Simy spent days preparing for her celebrated visitas. She usually engaged a popular Andalusian orchestra to play the latest tunes, so the soft sounds of the oud could mingle with the heady scent of smoldering sandalwood emanating from the incense burners she placed strategically throughout her long, narrow salon. On the day of the visita, music and incense drifted over her guests seated on the brightly covered divans that lined the walls. A platoon of waiters in white hooded robes called djellabahs and crimson fezzes (felt hats) circulated with trays of steaming mint tea, followed by a parade of pastries and sweets: knidlats, star-shaped cookies filled with marzipan; khibats, small "gazelle horns" stuffed with almond paste and glazed with pink or yellow icing; and translucent sections of candied lemons, oranges, or grapefruit for sandwiching between two diminutive pallébé cakes.

As a young girl on her way home from school, your aunt Victoria was often lured by the strains of Andalusian music to the site of a visita. She would brazenly sneak in and take a seat among the guests. If anyone inquired as to her presence, she would simply reply: "I have come to join my mother." She always managed to go home with enough pastries to share with her brothers and sisters! And Victoria grew up to be a discreet and elegant lady.

Your loving mother

Chicken Phyllo Triangles

(Pastelitos de Pollo)

Makes 25 to 30; serves 8

ez is renowned for b'stila, *a glorious creation of lightly sweetened saffron-scented chicken and ground almonds encased in layers of flaky, phyllo-like dough called* ouarka. *The crowning dish of the city's culinary repertoire inspired these Sephardic* pastelitos, *here accented with a touch of preserved lemon.*

2 tablespoons vegetable oil, plus additional for frying
1 onion, finely chopped
4 skinless chicken thighs
½ cup water
¼ teaspoon ground turmeric
¾ teaspoon ground ginger
½ teaspoon ground cinnamon
1 egg, lightly beaten
¾ teaspoon salt
⅛ teaspoon freshly ground black pepper
2 tablespoons very finely diced preserved lemon rind (page 20)
10 sprigs flat-leaf parsley, minced
5 (14 by 18-inch) sheets phyllo dough, thawed if frozen
Wedges of lemon, for serving

In a large heavy saucepan or a small Dutch oven, heat the 2 tablespoons oil over medium heat. Add the onion and cook, stirring occasionally, until golden, 6 to 8 minutes. Add the chicken thighs, water, turmeric, ginger, and cinnamon. Cover and cook until the chicken is tender, 20 to 25 minutes. With a slotted spoon, transfer the chicken to a bowl and set aside to cool. When cool enough to handle, bone and finely dice the chicken. You should have about 2 cups (approximately 12 ounces).

Return the cooking liquid to the stove and cook over medium heat until reduced by half, 10 to 15 minutes. Add the egg, salt, and pepper and stir

(continued)

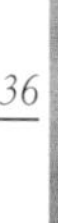

continuously until most of the cooking liquid evaporates, 12 to 15 minutes. Add the preserved lemon rind and the parsley. Combine with the diced chicken.

To make triangular-shaped *pastelitos*: Cover a work surface with a damp towel. Carefully unwrap the phyllo sheets and stack them on the towel. With the long edge of the phyllo toward you, and using a sharp knife, cut the stacked sheets into 6 equal sections to make 30 (3-inch-wide) strips. Stack the strips and cover them with the damp towel to prevent drying. Using one strip at a time, with the narrow edge facing you, place a scant tablespoon of filling about 1¾ inches from the bottom edge, and 1 inch from the left side of the strip. Fold the bottom right-hand corner up 45 degrees to partially cover the filling. Then fold the triangle straight up to align the left side of the triangle with the left side of the strip. Next, fold over the bottom left-hand corner to the right side of the strip. Continue folding in this manner, from side to side as you would a flag, gently pressing the filling as you work, to obtain a phyllo triangle about 3½ inches on a side. Tuck in the free end to seal. Repeat this process with the remaining phyllo strips until all the filling is used.

To make egg roll–shaped *pastelitos*: Proceed as above, cutting the stacked phyllo sheets into 4 equal sections to make 20 (4½-inch-wide) strips. Stack the strips and cover them with the damp towel to prevent drying. Using one strip at a time, with the narrow edge facing you, place a heaping tablespoon of filling about 1 inch from the bottom edge. Fold over the long sides, and roll up as you would an egg roll. Repeat until all the filling is used.

At this point, the *pastelitos* can be frozen in a single layer on a baking sheet and stored in a tightly sealed container for up to 3 months. Do not thaw before frying.

To cook, pour vegetable oil to a depth of 2 inches into a large heavy skillet and heat over medium heat until the oil reaches 325°, or until a piece of dough dropped into the oil sizzles instantly. Fry the *pastelitos* in batches until golden, 6 to 8 minutes, turning as needed to ensure even cooking. Drain well on paper towels. Serve immediately with wedges of lemon.

Soups and Salads

Tangier-Style White Bean and Chard Soup 41

Passover Fava Bean Soup 42

Dodie's Bean Soup with Preserved Lemons 45

Lentil and Garbanzo Bean Soup 46

Rosh Hashanah Cabbage Soup 48

Fried Eggplant 50

Tita's Tomato and Bell Pepper Salad 53

Fresh Fava Bean Salad 54

Danielle's Roasted Bell Peppers 57

Tomato Salad with Preserved Lemons 58

Cucumber and Lemon Salad 61

Chard Salad with Preserved Lemon 63

Fresh Fennel Salad 65

A Passover Seder

"When I was a boy in Algeria, all the family from out of town was invited. . . . The most solemn moment came during the evening Seder ceremony. . . . What opulence! On this special night we used the silverware engraved with our family initials and the special Passover china and its fifty-two place settings of delicate delft porcelain. The plates illustrated the tale of the Count of Monte Cristo. To this day, I still recall the design on my plate: It showed a swimmer in rags, staggering onto the beach with the caption: 'Dantès got up and took a few steps forward.'. . . At the end of the reading of the sacred Haggadah, our chorus of voices would intone the Had Gaddyah*."*

Translated from the personal memoirs of Armand Darmon, Kitty's maternal grandfather.

Armand Darmon, age 6, Oran, Algeria, 1896. (Photo courtesy Darmon family collection.)

Tangier-Style White Bean and Chard Soup

(Potaje Tangérois)

Serves 6

otaje Tangérois *is a specialty of the Jews of Tangier. Its Hispanic-French name attests to the cosmopolitan nature of the picturesque city on the northwest corner of Africa. Chard, an import from* Al Andalus, *has long been a staple of the Sephardic kitchen. Fresh warm bread is a must with this hearty soup.*

6 cups water or beef stock (page 4)
1 pound beef shank meat, cut into small cubes
1 small beef marrow bone
1½ cups small navy beans, soaked and drained (page 8)
2 bay leaves
8 cloves garlic, peeled
1 carrot, peeled and sliced
2 bunches Swiss chard (about 2 pounds)
2 teaspoons ground cumin
2 teaspoons sweet Hungarian paprika
2½ teaspoons salt
Ground cayenne pepper (optional)
5 to 6 tablespoons extra virgin olive oil
Harissa (page 12)

In a stockpot or large pot over high heat, combine the water, beef, marrow bone, beans, bay leaves, 6 of the garlic cloves, and the carrot. Bring to a rolling boil. With a slotted spoon, skim off the foam. Decrease the heat to medium, cover, and cook until the beans are tender, 1½ to 2 hours. Discard the bay leaves.

Trim the chard and cut the stems into 1-inch pieces. Cut the leaves into thin ribbons. Add to the beans. Cover and cook until the chard is tender, 10 to 12 minutes. Add the remaining 2 cloves garlic, cumin, paprika, salt, and cayenne. Cover and cook an additional 10 to 15 minutes.

To serve, ladle the soup into individual bowls and drizzle the olive oil over each serving. Pass the hot sauce at the table.

Passover Fava Bean Soup

(Soupe de Fèves de Pessah)

Serves 4

aman Darmon, Kitty's great-grandmother, always prepared this cilantro-laced fava bean soup for the Passover seder. In season, you can find fresh fava beans at farmers', Middle Eastern, or Italian markets. Substitute frozen baby lima beans for the favas, if you prefer.

4 pounds fresh fava beans, peeled and shelled (page 7)
1 potato, peeled and quartered
1 turnip, peeled and quartered
1 onion, quartered
6 cups beef stock (page 4)
1½ cups loosely packed cilantro leaves, plus additional for garnish
2 teaspoons salt
½ teaspoon freshly ground black pepper

In a large saucepan, combine the fava beans, potato, turnip, onion, and 2 cups of the stock. Bring to a low boil over medium heat. Cover and cook until the turnips are tender, 25 to 30 minutes. Allow to cool.

In a blender or food processor, purée the cooked vegetables and their cooking liquid in batches with the remaining 4 cups stock and the 1½ cups cilantro until smooth. Return the mixture to the saucepan. Season with the salt and pepper and heat through. Ladle the soup into individual bowls, garnish with the cilantro leaves, and serve hot.

My dear daughters,

How far removed our modern life is from that which prevailed in the Fez mellah two generations ago!

Jewish homes in the mellah differed from those in the Arab medina in that the former had windows that opened onto the street—an architectural element absent in Arab homes, where owners carefully sheltered the interior from public view.

Typically, Jewish homes had two stories. All the rooms faced an expansive atrium open to the sky, which allowed enough sunshine in to nurture an orange or lemon tree on a patch of earth below. Brightly painted wrought-iron railings of blue and gold surrounded the rooftop aperture. The home's terrace served as a social gathering place. Neighbors called from one rooftop to the next as they hung their laundry out to dry. In the summer, mellah dwellers slept under the stars to escape the sweltering heat of the city.

Decorative touches closely mirrored those of their Arab neighbors: floors and wainscotting of intricate, Moroccan zillij mosaics and ceilings of hand-painted wood or elaborately carved plaster. Heavy draperies of multicolored Genoese velvet could be released from their braided silk ties to afford the necessary privacy.

Children, whether married or unmarried, lived with their parents. My grandparents lived all their lives with my great-grandparents. Families of lesser means rented rooms in larger dwellings and shared common bathroom and laundry facilities. Each housewife kneaded the dough for her family's daily bread within the cramped confines of her living space. She let the dough rise on a wooden board placed just outside her door, until the tarah, the errand boy employed by the baker, carried it off to the communal oven.

Although such living arrangements constrained family privacy, the communal lifestyle within the grand homes of the mellah generated good humor and a spirit of solidarity. Rare disputes between tenants most frequently involved the disproportionate use of common facilities or the irksome behavior of a mischievous child. Impartial arbitrators helped settle such conflicts, dispensing a few glasses of mahiya (a distilled liquor made from dried figs, dates, raisins, or cherries) to assuage residual hard feelings. How this lifestyle differs from our present-day individualism. . . .

Your loving mother

Dodie's Bean Soup with Preserved Lemons

(Loubia de Dodie)

Serves 6

odie Hazan, a transplanted Fassia *(woman from Fez), who now resides in Montreal, claims this family favorite is not elegant enough to serve to guests, yet "everyone loves it!" Serve with a good crusty bread.*

1 tablespoon sweet Hungarian paprika
3 tablespoons virgin olive oil
2 cups dried baby lima beans, soaked and drained (page 8)
2 bay leaves
5 cups chicken stock (page 5)
12 cloves garlic, peeled
1 tablespoon ground cumin
2 large tomatoes, peeled, seeded (page 7), and coarsely chopped
2 tablespoons tomato paste
2 lamb or chicken sausages (about 4 ounces)
½ to ¾ preserved lemon rind (page 20)
⅛ teaspoon freshly ground black pepper
2 teaspoons salt

In a small bowl, blend the paprika with 2 tablespoons of the olive oil and mix until a paste forms. In a large pot over medium-high heat, cook the paprika paste, stirring until it darkens slightly, 2 to 3 minutes. Add the beans, bay leaves, and stock and stir to blend. Cover and bring to a boil for 2 to 3 minutes, then decrease the heat to low. Cook until the beans are tender, 1 to 1¼ hours. Discard the bay leaves. Add the garlic, cumin, tomatoes, and tomato paste and stir to blend. Cover and cook for 25 to 30 minutes.

Slice the sausages. In a small skillet, heat the remaining 1 tablespoon olive oil over medium-high heat. Add the sausages and cook, turning, until no longer pink, 4 to 5 minutes.

Dice the lemon rind and add it to taste to the beans, along with the pepper, salt, and sausage. Heat through and serve.

Lentil and Garbanzo Bean Soup

(Harira)

Serves 6

his hearty soup typifies the cross-cultural exchanges between Morocco's Arab and Jewish communities. In the month of Ramadan, Muslims traditionally break each day's fast with a steaming bowl of harira. *Jews savor the same nourishing dish to end their fast of Yom Kippur. Cooks employ different methods to thicken the soup. Some add a mixture of leavened dough and warm stock known as* tedouira. *Others use crushed angel hair pasta or a few tablespoons of rice; this version uses flour.*

2 tablespoons virgin olive oil
2 onions, sliced
4 celery stalks, diced
½ cup brown lentils, cleaned and picked over
7½ cups beef stock (page 4)
4 large tomatoes, peeled, seeded (page 7), and coarsely chopped
20 sprigs cilantro
15 sprigs flat-leaf parsley
1 tablespoon ground turmeric
1 teaspoon ground ginger
2 tablespoons raw long-grain rice
½ cup canned garbanzo beans, drained
1 teaspoon salt
¼ teaspoon freshly ground black pepper
3 tablespoons flour
Wedges of lemon, for serving

In a soup pot, heat the oil over medium-high heat. Add the onions and cook, stirring occasionally, until golden, 4 to 5 minutes. Add the celery, lentils, and 6½ cups of the stock. Cover tightly, and bring to a rolling boil. Cook until the celery is tender, 10 to 15 minutes. Decrease the heat to medium.

In a blender, combine ½ cup of the stock with the tomatoes, cilantro, parsley, turmeric, and ginger. Process until fairly smooth. Add to the lentils along with

the rice and the garbanzo beans. Continue cooking until the lentils are tender, 30 to 35 minutes. Season with the salt and pepper.

Five minutes before serving, bring the soup to a simmer. In a bowl, mix the flour with the remaining ½ cup stock to make a smooth paste. Add it to the soup, stirring continuously until it thickens somewhat. Do not boil. Serve immediately with wedges of lemon on the side.

Rosh Hashanah Cabbage Soup

(Soupe au Chou Vert de Rosh Hashanah)

Serves 6

he blare of the shofar (ram's horn), commemorating the sacrifice of Abraham, ushers in the two-day celebration of Rosh Hashanah. Friends and neighbors exchange greetings of "Shana Tovah!" ("Happy New Year!") In Fez, festivities include traditional dishes like this simple and flavorful cabbage soup.

1 small to medium green cabbage (about 1½ pounds)
3 potatoes, peeled and cut into ½-inch cubes
1 large onion, diced
1½ pounds beef stew meat, cut into 1-inch pieces
5 cups water
1½ teaspoons salt
¼ teaspoon freshly ground black pepper
½ teaspoon ground turmeric
10 sprigs cilantro, finely chopped, for garnish

Halve, core, and finely slice the cabbage. In a soup pot, combine the cabbage, potatoes, onion, beef, water, salt, pepper, and turmeric. Bring to a boil, uncovered, over high heat and skim off the foam. Decrease the heat to medium. Cover and cook until the meat is tender and the stock flavorful, 1½ to 2 hours. Sprinkle with cilantro and serve in individual soup bowls.

Pesach

Passover (Pesach)—a mid-spring holiday—is one of the most important High Holy Days of the Jewish calendar. It commemorates the ancient Hebrews' deliverance from Egyptian bondage. It also marks the end of the hardships of winter. Observant Jews eat only unleavened bread, called matzo, to remind them of their ancestors' hasty departure from Egypt.

The Seder tray, usually made of silver, must hold a number of symbolic ingredients: small "truffles" made of ground walnuts and dates called haroset, *to symbolize the brick and clay of the ancient Hebrews' toil in Egypt; two hard-boiled eggs, eaten on the second day of the feast, to symbolize the divine protection of the ancient Hebrews' first born; bitter herbs, such as fresh leaves of romaine lettuce, celery, or chervil, and a bowl of salted water to dip them in, to symbolize the bitterness of Egyptian bondage and the paucity of food in the desert; a piece of a lamb shoulder called* zeroua *as a symbol of Abraham's sacrifice; and six matzos known as* apikomenes.

The tray remains hidden under a beautiful, fringed silk shawl. Before lifting the shawl, the patriarch of the family must twice move the tray in a circular motion over the head of each guest while intoning, "Bibilo Yassano! Bibilo Yassano!" *the ancient chant that celebrates the Hebrews' release from Egyptian bondage.*

Passover Seder

Passover Fava Bean Soup (page 42)
Holiday Potato and Meat Pie (page 28)
Fresh Fava Bean Salad (page 54)
Roasted Lamb Shoulder (page 105)
or Tagine of Lamb with White Truffles (page 111)
Fresh, seasonal fruit
Assorted pastries and Mint Tea (page 172)

Fried Eggplant

(Aubergines Frites)

Serves 4

Eggplant originated on the Indian subcontinent. Its popularity spread west, and by the end of the first millennium, the purple globed vegetable was seducing sophisticated Persian palates. Later, Levantine Arabs and Jews would introduce it to the Iberian Peninsula, where it became such a favorite that eggplant dishes came to typify Sephardic cuisine. Substitute preserved kumquats for the lemon, if you prefer.

1 globe eggplant
Salt
⅓ cup virgin olive oil, for frying
3 cloves garlic, very finely minced
12 sprigs flat-leaf parsley, finely chopped
Finely minced rind of ½ preserved lemon (page 20)
3 tablespoons red wine vinegar or balsamic vinegar

Cut the unpeeled eggplant into ½-inch-thick slices. Set them on paper towels and sprinkle each slice very lightly with salt. Let the slices sweat for 15 minutes. Turn over and repeat the process. Rinse well under running water. Pat dry with paper towels and set aside.

Line a baking sheet with a double layer of paper towels. In a large skillet, heat 2 tablespoons of the oil over medium-high heat. Add as many eggplant slices as will fit in a single uncrowded layer, and fry, turning once, until they are lightly browned on each side, 6 to 8 minutes. Fry the remaining slices, adding oil as needed. Drain on the paper towels.

When cool, arrange the slices on a serving platter. Sprinkle with the garlic, parsley, preserved lemon rind, and vinegar. Serve at room temperature. The eggplant will keep for up to a week in an airtight container in the refrigerator. Bring to room temperature before serving.

Tita's Tomato and Bell Pepper Salad

(FRITA DE TITA)

Serves 6

rita, chouchouka, chakchouka—*however they call it, Moroccan Jews have a particular fondness for this refreshing salad of tomatoes and roasted peppers. Kitty's great-aunt Tita always made enough to have some left over for a light supper—eggs gently poached in a nest of warm* frita. *Use a variety of green, yellow, and red peppers for a more colorful dish.*

4 bell peppers, roasted and seeded (page 7)
2 tablespoons virgin olive oil
4 tomatoes, peeled, seeded (page 7), and coarsely diced
2 cloves garlic, minced
½ teaspoon sugar
1 tablespoon tomato paste
¾ teaspoon salt
1 teaspoon sweet Hungarian paprika

Cut the peppers into ½-inch strips. Set aside in a colander to drain.

In a large skillet, heat the olive oil over medium heat. Add the tomatoes, garlic, sugar, and tomato paste. Cook, uncovered, lightly pressing on the tomatoes, until most of the liquid evaporates, 12 to 15 minutes. Add the drained peppers and season with the salt and paprika. Cover and cook, stirring occasionally, until the mixture thickens, 10 to 15 minutes. Remove the lid. Continue cooking until most of the liquid evaporates, another 10 to 12 minutes.

Let cool and serve at room temperature. *Frita* lasts for up to 4 or 5 days in an airtight container in the refrigerator. Bring to room temperature before serving.

Fresh Fava Bean Salad

(Salade de Févettes)

Serves 4

hen woven straw baskets at the local souk (open-air market) overflow with tender fava beans, it is a sure sign of spring. Happily, the arrival of the most popular member of the pulse family coincides with the feast of Passover, allowing this delightful salad to make its appearance.

8 ounces (about 1½ cups) shelled and peeled fava beans (page 7), with 3 to 4 tender pods reserved
2 tablespoons extra virgin olive oil
1 teaspoon sweet Hungarian paprika
1½ teaspoons ground cumin
3 cloves garlic, minced
¼ cup water
3 tablespoons freshly squeezed lemon juice
10 cilantro sprigs, finely chopped
¾ teaspoon salt
Cilantro leaves, for garnish

String the reserved bean pods and cut them into ½-inch pieces.

In a large skillet over medium heat, combine the olive oil, paprika, cumin, and garlic. Cook until the mixture begins to foam, 2 to 3 minutes. Add the beans, pods, and water. Cook, stirring, until the beans are tender but not soft, 8 to 10 minutes. Add the lemon juice, chopped cilantro, and salt. Cook, stirring, for 1 to 2 minutes.

Transfer the beans to a serving dish and allow to cool. Garnish with cilantro leaves and serve at room temperature. This salad lasts for 2 to 3 days in an airtight container in the refrigerator. Bring to room temperature before serving.

Danielle's Roasted Bell Peppers

(Les Poivrons de Danielle)

Serves 4

anielle's daughters always request a pound or two of their mother's twice-cooked peppers whenever she visits them in Paris. Use them as a relish or as a filling for sandwiches.

5 red bell peppers (about 2 pounds)
3 tablespoons extra virgin olive oil
4 cloves garlic, thinly sliced
½ teaspoon salt

Preheat the broiler and line a baking sheet with aluminum foil. Cut the peppers along the grooves into 5 or 6 lobes. Place, skin side up, on the prepared baking sheet. Broil until the skins blister evenly, 8 to 10 minutes. Transfer to a bowl and cover tightly with plastic wrap. When cool, peel and seed the peppers.

In a large skillet, heat the olive oil over medium heat. Add the garlic and cook, stirring occasionally, until it turns golden, 3 to 4 minutes. Add the peppers and fry for 3 to 4 minutes on each side. Transfer to a colander to drain.

Arrange the peppers on a serving dish as if they were petals of a flower. Sprinkle with the salt and the fried garlic. Serve at room temperature. The peppers will keep for up to a week in an airtight container in the refrigerator. Bring to room temperature before serving.

Tomato Salad with Preserved Lemons

(Salade de Tomates aux Citrons Confits)

Serves 4

refreshing simplicity characterizes this mouthwatering combination of vine-ripened tomatoes and preserved lemons. Serve it as a salad or as an unusual topping for crostini or bruschetta. You'll need to prepare the lemons several weeks ahead of time.

4 vine-ripened tomatoes, peeled, seeded (page 7), and cubed
2 to 4 teaspoons diced preserved lemon rind (page 20)
⅛ teaspoon salt
1 tablespoon red wine vinegar or balsamic vinegar
4 or 5 green olives, sliced, or 8 whole dry-cured black olives
1 small jalapeño pepper, seeded, cored,
and very finely diced (optional)

Place the tomatoes in a colander and drain for 30 minutes.

In a small bowl, combine the tomatoes, lemon rind to taste, salt, vinegar, olives, and jalapeño and mix thoroughly. Serve at room temperature.

Cucumber and Lemon Salad

(Salade de Concombres et Citrons)

Serves 4

he cucumber remains as popular today as it was at the time of the ancient Hebrews. This cool salad provides welcome relief on sweltering summer days.

2 lemons
½ teaspoon salt
2 Japanese or English cucumbers, peeled, seeded, and very thinly sliced
1 sweet onion, very thinly sliced
3 tablespoons extra virgin olive oil
¼ teaspoon freshly ground black pepper
1 teaspoon dried oregano, lightly crushed

Peel and section the lemons, removing the seeds and white pith. Coarsely dice the sections. Transfer to a bowl and toss with the salt.

In a serving dish, layer the cucumbers, then the onion, and finally the lemon pieces. In a small bowl, whisk together the olive oil, pepper, and oregano. Spoon over the dish and serve.

La Mimouna

La Mimouna, a celebration held on the last evening of Passover, is unique to Moroccan Sephardim. Local tradition dictates that Muslim families offer their Jewish friends or neighbors a lump of starter dough, eliminated from Sephardic pantries during the weeklong celebration of Passover.

Dinner

Couscous with Onion and Raisin Confit (page 120)
Roasted Chicken with Orange Juice (page 83)
Fresh, seasonal fruit
Currant Preserves (page 166)
Sephardic Pancakes (page 78) or assorted pastries and Mint Tea (page 172)

Dona Darmon (née Hassan), Kitty's great-grandmother, Oran, Algeria, circa 1900. (Photo courtesy Scémama family collection.)

Chard Salad with Preserved Lemon

(Blettes aux Citrons Confits)

Serves 8

*n season, a salad of Swiss chard is part of every Shabbat meal. Chard is one of the vegetables that receives a special* beraha *(blessing) during Passover.* Fassis *(Fez natives) create a light snack by sandwiching a spoonful of the tangy salad between two pieces of crisp matzo. Substitute preserved kumquats (page 18) for the lemon, if you prefer.*

- 3 tablespoons virgin olive oil
- 5 cloves garlic, minced
- 1 (12-ounce) bunch red chard, stemmed and chopped
- 1 (12-ounce) bunch white chard, stemmed and chopped
- Rind of ¼ preserved lemon (page 20), finely diced
- 1 tablespoon freshly squeezed lemon juice
- ½ teaspoon salt
- ⅛ teaspoon freshly ground black pepper
- Lemon slices, for garnish

Heat the oil in a large skillet over medium-high heat. Add the garlic and cook, stirring occasionally until golden, 2 to 3 minutes. Add the chard leaves, a handful at a time. Using 2 wooden spoons, toss them until wilted, 3 to 4 minutes. Proceed in this manner until all the leaves are used. Add the lemon rind, lemon juice, salt, and pepper. Toss to blend and transfer to a serving bowl. Garnish with lemon slices and serve at room temperature.

Fresh Fennel Salad

(Salade de Fenouil Cru)

Serves 4

ransform this anise-scented summer salad into a quick and light luncheon by adding chunks of canned tuna.

2 fennel bulbs, trimmed
Juice of 1 lemon
3 tablespoons extra virgin olive oil
½ teaspoon salt
½ teaspoon freshly ground black pepper
1 sweet onion, thinly sliced
1 stalk celery, finely diced
10 dry-cured black olives, for garnish

Slice the fennel bulbs into thin rings. In a small bowl, whisk together the lemon juice, olive oil, salt, and pepper.

In a bowl, combine the fennel rings, onion slices, and celery. Add the dressing and toss to coat evenly. Garnish with the olives and serve.

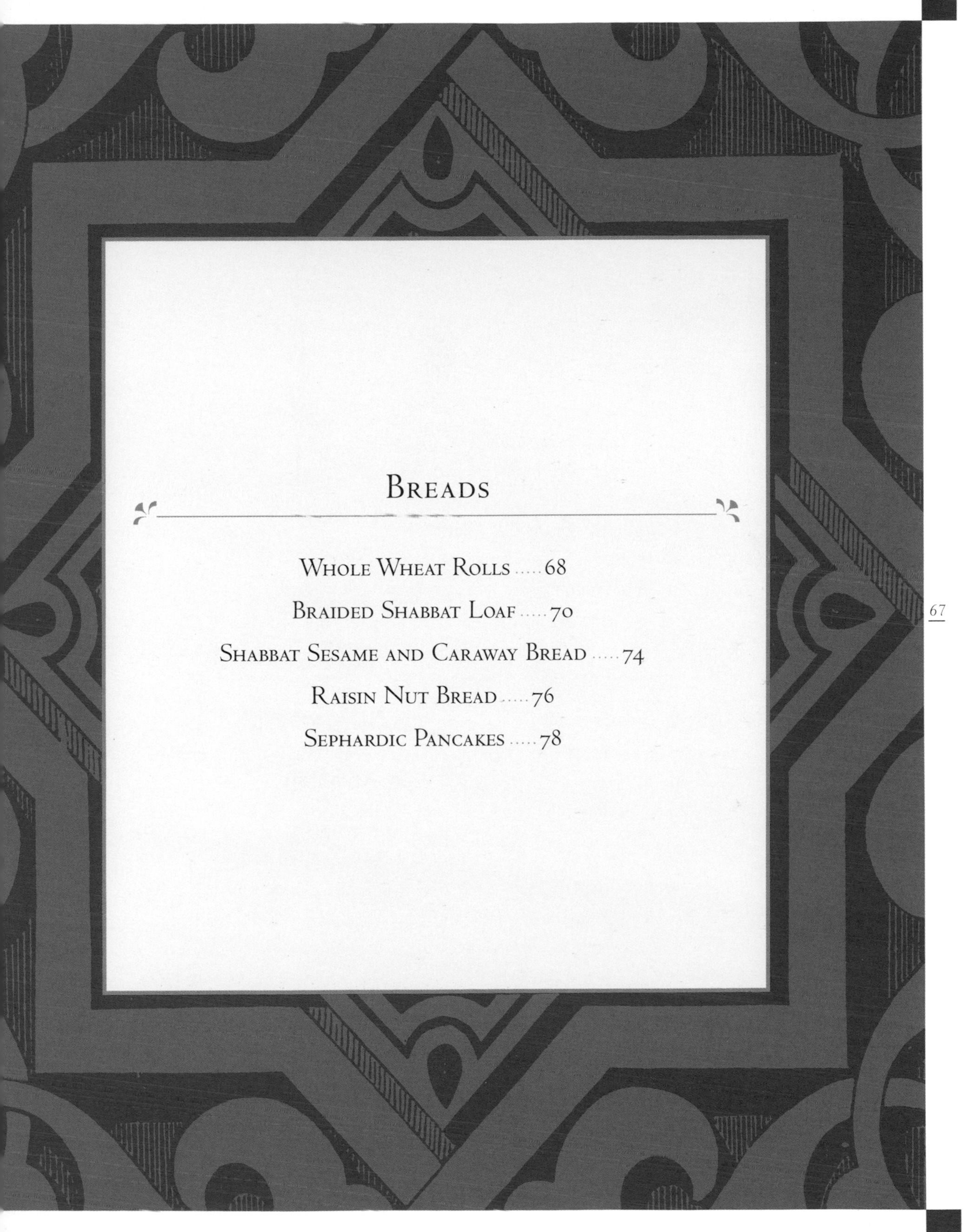

Breads

Whole Wheat Rolls 68

Braided Shabbat Loaf 70

Shabbat Sesame and Caraway Bread 74

Raisin Nut Bread 76

Sephardic Pancakes 78

Whole Wheat Rolls

(Petits Pains Complets)

Makes 12

any Moroccan housewives still make their own bread, leavening with a lump of dough from the previous day's batch. A few bake the bread at home, but they usually utilize the neighborhood ferrane *(public oven).*

2 envelopes active dry yeast
1 teaspoon sugar
2½ cups warm water (105 to 110°)
6 cups stone-ground whole wheat flour
1 teaspoon salt
1 egg, lightly beaten (optional)
⅓ cup fine semolina, for dusting
Sesame seeds, caraway seeds, or aniseeds (optional), for garnish

In a small bowl, mix the yeast and sugar with ½ cup of the water. Stir gently and set aside until the mixture begins to bubble, 10 to 12 minutes.

In a large, shallow bowl, combine the flour and salt. Make a well in the center. Add the yeast mixture and the egg and mix until combined. Knead, adding the remaining water as necessary to make a smooth, elastic dough, 12 to 15 minutes. Shape the dough into a ball, and let it rest for 2 to 3 minutes. Knead again vigorously for 1 minute.

Generously sprinkle 2 baking sheets with semolina. Divide the dough into 12 equal parts. Shape each part into a ball and set it on the baking sheet. Using your fingers, flatten each ball to a diameter of 3 to 3½ inches. Sprinkle with seeds and prick the centers several times with the tines of a fork. Cover with a clean cloth. Let rise in a warm (about 75°), dry place, away from drafts, until they double in size, 1 to 1½ hours.

Preheat the oven to 400°. Bake on the center rack until golden brown, 15 to 18 minutes. Cool briefly on wire racks and serve warm. (Pictured on opposite page, left.)

Braided Shabbat Loaf

(Challa)

Makes 1 loaf

n a weekly ritual, Sephardic housewives burned an olive-sized lump of Shabbat dough, called a halla, *to symbolize the tithe once paid to Levitical priests in biblical times. Bread is the subject of a special* beraha *(blessing) on the Shabbat. Two braided loaves are placed on the table to symbolize the tablets of the Law.*

2 envelopes active dry yeast
2 tablespoons plus 1 teaspoon sugar
1½ to 1¾ cups warm water (100 to 105°)
6 cups unbleached all-purpose flour
2 teaspoons salt
3 eggs
4 tablespoons sunflower oil
⅓ cup fine semolina, for dusting
3 tablespoons sesame seeds, toasted (page 8)

In a small bowl, mix the yeast and sugar with ½ cup of the water. Stir gently and set aside until the mixture begins to bubble, 10 to 12 minutes.

In a large, shallow bowl, combine the flour and the salt. Make a well in the center. Add the yeast mixture, 2 of the eggs, and the oil and mix to combine. Knead, adding the remaining water as necessary to make a smooth, elastic dough, 12 to 15 minutes.

Shape the dough into a ball and transfer to a lightly oiled bowl. Cover with a clean towel. Let rise in a warm (about 75°), dry place, away from drafts, until it doubles in size, 1 to 1½ hours.

Generously sprinkle a baking sheet with semolina. On the baking sheet, stretch the risen dough into a loaf about 10 inches long. Beginning 1 inch from the top end, using a serrated knife, cut the loaf lengthwise into three equal strips. Braid the strips, pinching the bottom end with your fingers to seal. Let rise, covered with a clean towel, for 1 hour.

Preheat the oven to 425°. Lightly beat the remaining egg with 1 tablespoon water. Brush the loaf with the egg wash and sprinkle generously with sesame seeds.

Bake on the center rack for 10 minutes. Decrease the heat to 400° and bake until golden brown, 18 to 20 minutes. Cool briefly on a wire rack and serve. (Pictured on page 69, bottom right.) ❧

Shavuot

Shavuot, which translates as "weeks," is a festival held exactly seven weeks after Passover. On this day, Jews celebrate the gift of the Torah to Moses on Mount Sinai. Jews give thanks for the first harvest of fruits. Some families mark the occasion by preparing dishes containing dairy products.

Menu

Holiday Potato and Meat Pie (page 28)
Assorted salads
Fresh, seasonal fruit
Assorted pastries and Mint Tea (page 172)

Kitty's great-aunt and culinary mentor, Suzanne Coriat (née Darmon), Oran, Algeria, circa 1917.

My darling daughters,

I'm sitting here on our front porch with "Shems el Hachiya" ("The Afternoon Sun"), one of my favorite pieces of Andalusian music, playing on the radio. The tune brings back memories of grandfather Aflalo (see the picture I've enclosed: he's on the left side of the photo, sitting cross-legged behind the tea tray). He was a great musician and one of those rare Jews in Morocco, along with Rabbi David Bouzaglou, who possessed an intimate knowledge of Andalusian music. This music is to the Maghreb what classical music is to the Western world. I can still see grandfather Aflalo making notations on his sheet music as he switched among his three violins. Musicians from all over Morocco respected his expertise and often sought him out for advice. One of them, Abdelkrim Raiss, went on to become a performer of international renown. Full orchestras often packed our expansive living room. It was all very exciting for our family, especially on the eve of a live radio performance. This, of course, was before the advent of television. I'll try to have a tape made from a recording of one of his concerts, and send a copy to you.

Your loving mother

Musical interlude with the Aflalo and Benzimra families, Fez, circa 1932. (Photo courtesy of Aflalo-Benzimra family collection.)

Shabbat Sesame and Caraway Bread

(Khbiza Del Zrarehe)

Makes 4 loaves

or Sephardic families of modest means, homemade bread was often the only baked good served on Shabbat. More extravagant and relatively expensive sweet pastries were reserved for major feast days. To add variety to the Shabbat meal with little additional cost, housewives incorporated sesame, anise, or caraway seeds into their dough.

2 envelopes active dry yeast
1 teaspoon sugar
1¾ cups warm water (100 to 105°)
6 cups unbleached all-purpose flour
1 teaspoon salt
3 tablespoons sesame seeds, toasted (page 8)
2 tablespoons caraway seeds or aniseeds, toasted (page 8)
3 tablespoons sunflower oil
⅓ cup fine semolina, for dusting
1 egg, lightly beaten with 1 tablespoon water, for egg wash (optional)

In a small bowl, mix the yeast and sugar with ¼ cup of the water. Stir gently and set aside until the mixture begins to bubble, 10 to 12 minutes.

In a large shallow bowl, combine the flour, salt, sesame seeds, and caraway seeds. Make a well in the center. Add the yeast mixture, oil, and 1 cup of the water and mix to combine. Knead, adding the remaining ½ cup water as needed, to make a smooth, elastic dough, 10 to 12 minutes. Shape into a ball, and let it rest for 5 to 10 minutes. Knead again vigorously for 1 minute.

Lightly grease 2 large baking sheets and generously sprinkle them with semolina. Divide the dough into 4 equal parts. Shape each one into a ball. On a lightly floured surface, flatten each ball to about 7 inches in diameter with a rolling pin. Place 2 rounds of dough on each sheet and cover with a clean cloth. Let rise in a warm (about 75°), dry place, away from drafts, until they double in size, about 1 hour.

Preheat the oven to 400°. Prick the center of each loaf with a fork and let rise for 10 minutes. Lightly brush each round with egg wash.

Place 1 baking sheet at a time on the center rack and bake until golden brown, 22 to 25 minutes. Cool briefly on wire racks and serve. (Pictured on page 69, upper right.)

Raisin Nut Bread

(Pain aux Raisins Secs et aux Noix)

Makes 2 loaves

lentiful, assorted pastries and confections highlight the joyful celebration of Purim. This sweet, flower-shaped bread concealing a cache of nuts and raisins is a special Purim treat.

2 envelopes active dry yeast
1 cup sugar
1¾ cups warm water (100 to 105°)
3 eggs
6 cups unbleached all-purpose flour
1 teaspoon salt
½ cup vegetable oil
½ cup raisins, plumped in warm water and drained
½ cup walnut pieces
⅓ cup fine semolina, for dusting
1 tablespoon cold water

In a small bowl, mix the yeast and 1 teaspoon of the sugar with ¼ cup of the water. Stir gently and set aside until the mixture begins to bubble, 10 to 12 minutes.

In a small bowl, lightly beat 2 of the eggs.

In a large shallow bowl, combine the flour, salt, and remaining sugar. Make a well in the center. Add the yeast mixture, eggs, oil, and 1 cup of the water and mix well. Knead, adding the remaining ½ cup water as needed, to make a smooth, elastic dough, 10 to 12 minutes. Shape into a ball, and let it rest for 5 to 10 minutes. Knead again vigorously for 1 minute.

In a small bowl, combine the raisins and nuts.

Divide the dough into 4 equal parts and shape each into a ball. On a lightly floured surface, flatten each ball to 8 inches in diameter with a rolling pin.

Lightly oil 2 large baking sheets with vegetable oil and generously dust them with semolina. Place a dough round on each pan. Sprinkle half of the raisin-nut mixture in the center of each round. Cover with a second round and seal the edges.

Using a knife, make a number of 3-inch-long cuts, forming strips around the perimeter of the loaf at ½-inch intervals. With your fingers, pinch and seal the strips in groups of three to give the loaf a flowerlike appearance.

Cover each pan with a clean cloth. Let rise in a warm (about 75°), dry place, away from drafts, until they double in size, about 1½ hours.

Preheat the oven to 400°. In a small bowl, beat the remaining egg with the cold water. Lightly brush each loaf with the egg wash and prick the center with a fork. Let rise for 10 minutes.

Bake on the center rack until golden brown, 25 to 30 minutes. Cool briefly on wire racks and serve. (Pictured on page 69, middle right.)

Sephardic Pancakes

(MAFLETA)

Makes about 15; serves 6

he preparation of mafleta *was a team effort in many Sephardic households. Plates of warm* mafleta *dripping with honey and butter, were de rigueur on the feast of La Mimouna. The following day, leftovers were shredded into bite-sized pieces, and cooked in melted butter and sugar until lightly caramelized. Mafleta is traditionally served with mint tea.*

2 cups all-purpose flour
¼ teaspoon salt
¾ cup plus 2 tablespoons water
½ cup vegetable oil, for frying
Honey or sugar
½ cup unsalted butter or margarine
¼ cup sugar or honey
2 teaspoons orange blossom water (page 6)

In a bowl, combine the flour, salt, and water. Transfer to a lightly floured surface and knead until you have a breadlike dough, 2 to 3 minutes. Break the dough into 15 portions of equal size. Lightly oil a work surface. Using your fingertips, spread each ball of dough to a diameter of about 7 inches.

Heat 2 tablespoons of the oil in a large skillet over medium-high heat. Immediately fry the first mafleta until golden on the first side, 2½ to 3 minutes. Flip and fry until golden on the second side, 2½ to 3 minutes. Leave the mafleta in the pan, and set a second uncooked mafleta on top of the first. Add oil as needed. Flip to allow the new addition to cook until golden, 2 to 2½ minutes. (All mafleta, except the first, will cook on one side only). Set another mafleta on top of the uppermost one. Flip again and cook. Add another mafleta to the stack. Again, add oil as needed. Flip and cook the new one. Continue adding and flipping mafleta, until you have a stack of 15. At this point, you can serve the hot mafleta whole with honey or sugar on the side.

Break any leftover mafleta into bite-sized pieces. In a large skillet, combine the butter, sugar, and orange blossom water and cook over medium-high heat until the butter is melted. Add the mafleta and toss to coat. Cook until lightly caramelized, 10 to 12 minutes. Serve immediately and eat with your fingers.

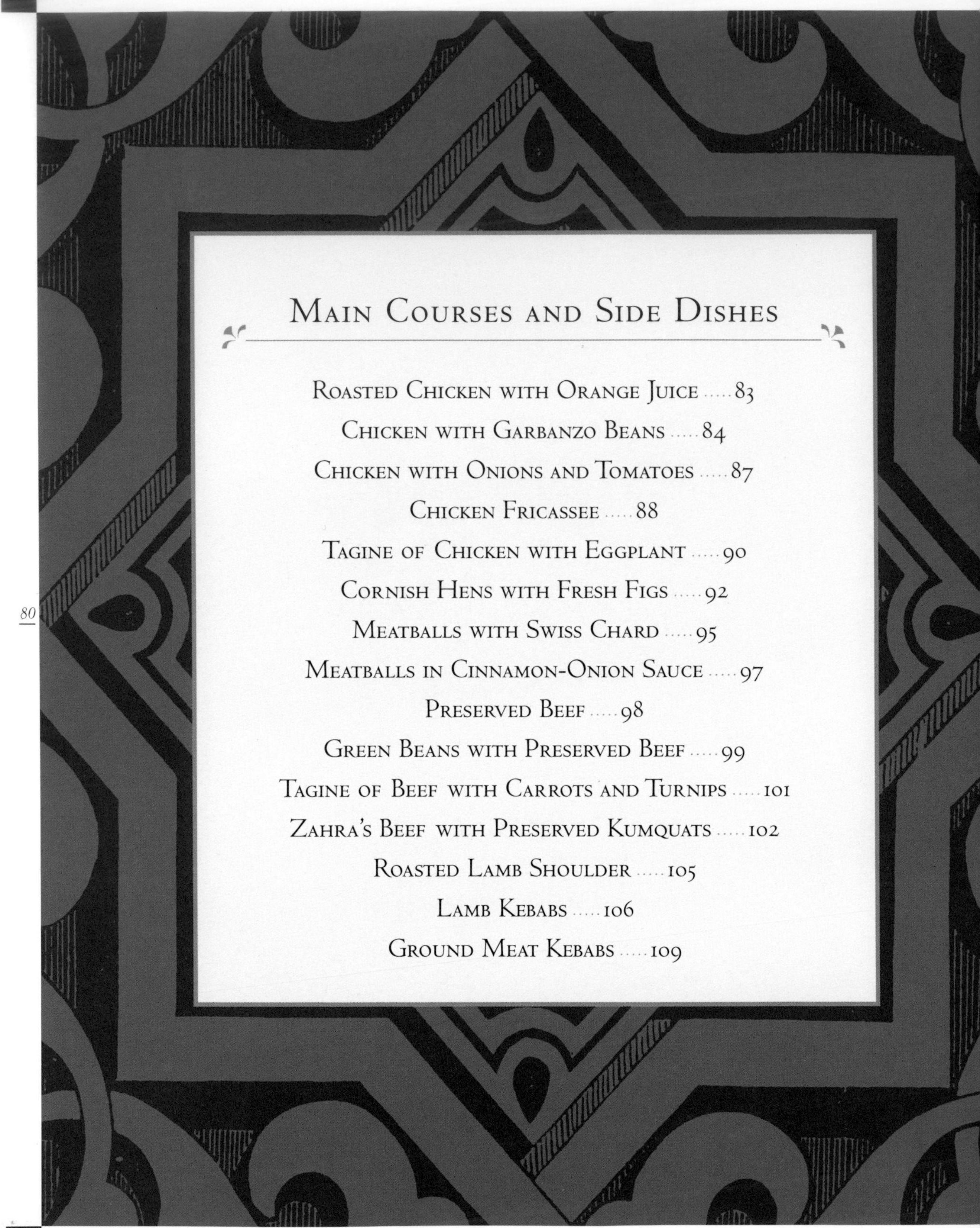

Main Courses and Side Dishes

Roasted Chicken with Orange Juice 83

Chicken with Garbanzo Beans 84

Chicken with Onions and Tomatoes 87

Chicken Fricassee 88

Tagine of Chicken with Eggplant 90

Cornish Hens with Fresh Figs 92

Meatballs with Swiss Chard 95

Meatballs in Cinnamon-Onion Sauce 97

Preserved Beef 98

Green Beans with Preserved Beef 99

Tagine of Beef with Carrots and Turnips 101

Zahra's Beef with Preserved Kumquats 102

Roasted Lamb Shoulder 105

Lamb Kebabs 106

Ground Meat Kebabs 109

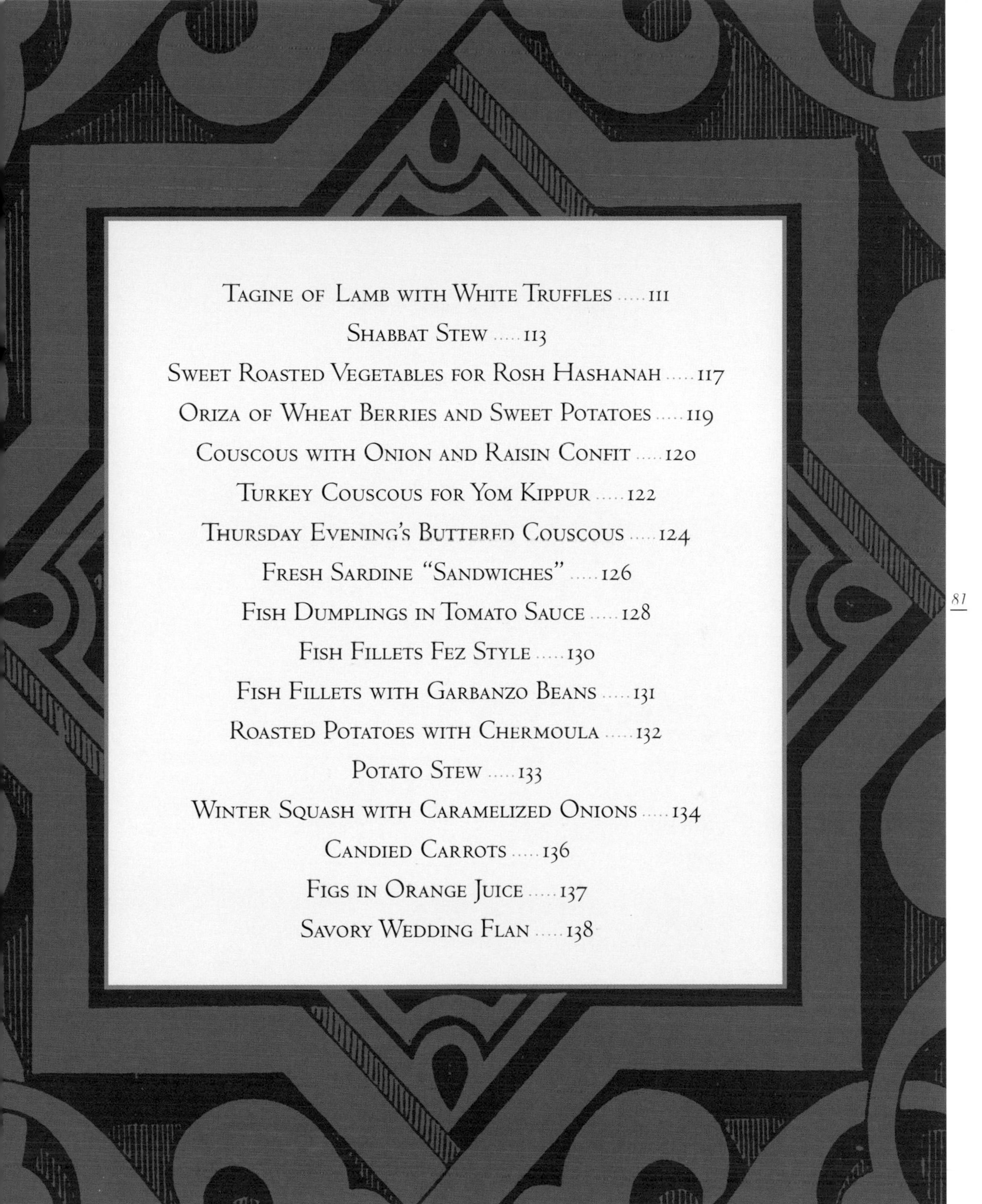

Tagine of Lamb with White Truffles 111

Shabbat Stew 113

Sweet Roasted Vegetables for Rosh Hashanah 117

Oriza of Wheat Berries and Sweet Potatoes 119

Couscous with Onion and Raisin Confit 120

Turkey Couscous for Yom Kippur 122

Thursday Evening's Buttered Couscous 124

Fresh Sardine "Sandwiches" 126

Fish Dumplings in Tomato Sauce 128

Fish Fillets Fez Style 130

Fish Fillets with Garbanzo Beans 131

Roasted Potatoes with Chermoula 132

Potato Stew 133

Winter Squash with Caramelized Onions 134

Candied Carrots 136

Figs in Orange Juice 137

Savory Wedding Flan 138

Roasted Chicken with Orange Juice

(Poulet Rôti au Jus d'Orange)

Serves 4

ucculent, slow-roasted chicken is a highlight of a Sephardic luncheon chez *Danielle. She surrounds her moist, tender bird with either a ring of glistening candied carrots or baked figs.*

2 cups freshly squeezed orange juice
2 chicken bouillon cubes, crumbled
1 (4-pound) roasting chicken, cleaned and patted dry
Salt and freshly ground black pepper

Preheat the oven to 325°. In a small bowl, combine the orange juice with the bouillon cubes and whisk to dissolve the cubes.

Place the chicken in a roasting pan and season the cavity with salt and pepper. Spoon half of the juice mixture over and into the cavity of the bird. Roast, basting occasionally with the remaining juice mixture, until the legs move easily, 2 to 2¼ hours.

Let the chicken rest for 10 minutes before carving. Serve the chicken hot with the pan juices on the side.

Chicken with Garbanzo Beans

(Pollo con Garbanzos)

Serves 4

ooks from the northern city of Tétouan prepare this special dish on Sukkoth, the Feast of the Tabernacles. Serve it immediately, so your guests can enjoy its fleeting, soufflé-like appearance. Crusty fresh bread is a great accompaniment.

5 tablespoons virgin olive oil
1 onion, finely diced
1 teaspoon sweet Hungarian paprika
1 teaspoon ground turmeric
2 cloves garlic, minced
8 skinless chicken thighs
¾ cup chicken stock (page 5) or water
4 eggs, lightly beaten
2 teaspoons salt
⅛ teaspoon freshly ground black pepper
1 teaspoon ground cinnamon
⅛ teaspoon ground cayenne pepper (optional)
1 (14¼-ounce) can garbanzo beans, drained
1 red bell pepper, roasted (page 7) and finely diced
15 sprigs flat-leaf parsley, minced

In an ovenproof skillet, heat 2 tablespoons of the oil over medium-high heat. Add the onion and cook, stirring occasionally, until lightly browned, 6 to 8 minutes.

Meanwhile, in a large bowl, combine the remaining 3 tablespoons oil, paprika, turmeric, and garlic. Stir to blend. Coat each piece of chicken with the mixture, and add to the onions. Cook, turning occasionally, until browned, 4 to 5 minutes. Add the stock, cover, and decrease the heat to medium. Cook until the chicken is tender, 30 to 35 minutes. Using tongs, transfer the chicken to a bowl. Reserve the pan juices.

Preheat the oven to 425°.

In a bowl, combine the eggs, salt, pepper, cinnamon, cayenne, garbanzo beans, bell pepper, and minced parsley. Add the reserved pan juices to the egg mixture and blend well with a wooden spoon. Pour the mixture back into the skillet and top with the chicken.

Bake until the eggs puff up, 15 to 20 minutes. Serve immediately.

Purim

The two-day celebration of Purim, Feast of the Lots (Feast of Esther) takes place on the fourteenth of Adar. It celebrates the defeat of Hamman and his fellow plotters, who planned to annihilate ancient Babylon's Jewish population. Queen Esther and her uncle Mordechai helped thwart the secret attack, the date of which had been determined by lots. Generations of Moroccan Jews feasted on a special species of shad called shabel *(*alose *in French), which once flourished in the estuary of Morocco's large rivers. Today, sardines replace the original delicacy.*

Dinner

FRESH SARDINE "SANDWICHES" (PAGE 126)
GREEN BEANS WITH PRESERVED BEEF (PAGE 99)
FRESH, SEASONAL FRUIT
ASSORTED PASTRIES AND MINT TEA (PAGE 172)

Sephardic men of Debdou, southern Morocco, circa 1900. (Photo courtesy Mamane family collection. Gift to Diaspora Museum, Tel Aviv, Israel.)

Chicken with Onions and Tomatoes

(Poulet aux Oignons et aux Tomates)

Serves 4

*he jamlike, honey-flavored sauce in this delightful dish begs for sops of warm, crusty bread. The dried ginger (fresh ginger is never used in Moroccan cuisine) reflects the culinary influence of the Arabs, who introduced the fragrant rhizome into North Africa at the end of the seventh century.*

¼ cup virgin olive oil
8 to 10 chicken pieces
3 large onions, thinly sliced
4 large tomatoes, peeled, seeded (page 7), and coarsely chopped
2 tablespoons honey
¼ teaspoon freshly ground black pepper
1¼ teaspoons ground ginger
8 threads Spanish saffron, toasted and crushed (page 7)
1½ teaspoons salt
Toasted almonds (page 8), for garnish

In a small Dutch oven, heat the oil over medium-high heat. Add the chicken and cook, turning occasionally, until golden on all sides, 5 to 6 minutes. Remove from the pan and set aside.

Preheat the oven to 350°.

Add the onions to the oil remaining in the pan. Cook, stirring occasionally, until they are lightly browned, 10 to 12 minutes. Add the tomatoes, honey, pepper, ginger, and saffron and decrease the heat to medium. Cook, stirring occasionally, until the sauce thickens somewhat, 15 to 20 minutes. Add the salt and the reserved chicken pieces. Transfer to the oven and bake until the chicken is tender, 40 to 45 minutes. Sprinkle with the almonds and serve.

Chicken Fricassee

(Fricasada de Pollo)

Serves 4

oroccan housewives purchase live chickens from a kosher butcher. Traditionally, no part of the bird goes to waste—hearts, livers, and gizzards are incorporated into fricasada de pollo. *We use only the breast and livers in the following recipe, however. In Tétouan, during the festival of Rosh Hashanah, the seasonal vegetables included in* fricasada *are meant to symbolize the hope for a bountiful new year. In the city of Fez, the dish is most common on Yom Kippur, when one chicken is sacrificed for each member of the family.*

2 tablespoons virgin olive oil
1 onion, diced
1 large leek, white part only, sliced and rinsed under running water
2 carrots, peeled and thinly sliced
2 boneless skinless chicken breasts, cut into 1-inch cubes
1 cup freshly squeezed orange juice
¼ teaspoon ground nutmeg
2 yellow zucchini or summer squash, peeled and diced
2 green zucchini, peeled and diced
1 potato, peeled and diced
½ cup frozen petite green peas
1 teaspoon salt
¼ teaspoon freshly ground black pepper
1 pound chicken livers, cleaned and patted dry
Grated orange zest, for garnish

In a large skillet, heat the oil over medium-high heat. Add the onion and cook, stirring occasionally, until wilted, 5 to 6 minutes. Add the leek, carrots, and chicken. Cook, stirring, until the chicken is browned, 5 to 6 minutes. Add ½ cup of the orange juice and the nutmeg. Cover and cook until the carrots are tender, 8 to 10 minutes. Add the squashes and potato. Cover and cook until the potato is tender, 15 to 18 minutes. Add the peas and season with ¾ teaspoon of the salt and ⅛ teaspoon of the pepper. Preheat the oven to 200°.

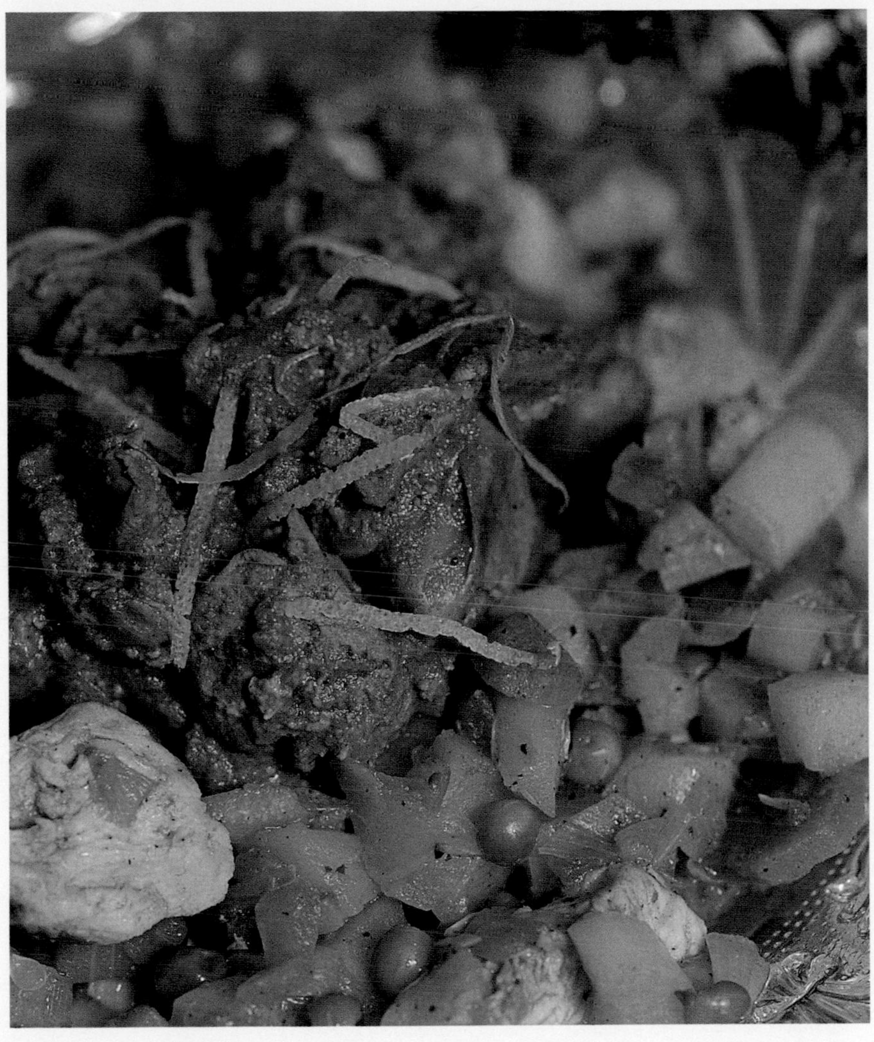

Using a slotted spoon, transfer the vegetables and chicken to an ovenproof serving platter and keep warm in the oven.

Cut each chicken liver into 3 equal pieces. Add the livers, the remaining ½ cup orange juice, ¼ teaspoon salt, and ⅛ teaspoon pepper to the skillet. Cook over medium heat until the livers are tender, 8 to 10 minutes.

Arrange the vegetables and chicken in a ring around the serving platter. Place the livers in the center. Spoon the pan juices over the dish, garnish with the orange zest, and serve.

Tagine of Chicken with Eggplant

(Baraniya)

Serves 6

araniya (al-moroniya, *as it is called in Tangier) is mentioned in Arab texts of the ninth century. According to Los Angeles–based food historian Charles Perry, the dish was named for Boran, the daughter of Persian vizier Al Mahmun, whose elaborate wedding to a wealthy caliph became legendary for its extravagance. Ingenious palace chefs created the subtle flavors of* baraniya *for the occasion. The recipe would seduce the medieval Islamic world, including* Al Andalus, *and eventually, North Africa. Moroccan Jews made it a tradition for the celebration of Yom Kippur.*

2 globe eggplants, peeled and cut into ¼-inch-thick slices
½ cup vegetable oil
3 cloves garlic, minced
10 to 12 chicken pieces
3 large onions, thinly sliced
2 tablespoons sugar or honey
1 tablespoon "Top of the Shop" Spice Blend (page 23)
¼ cup chicken stock (page 5)
8 threads Spanish saffron, toasted and crushed (page 7)
2 teaspoons salt
¼ teaspoon freshly ground black pepper

Place the eggplant slices on a layer of paper towels. Sprinkle lightly with salt. Let sweat for 10 minutes and pat dry with paper towels. Turn the slices over, and repeat on the other side. Rinse them quickly under running water and pat dry.

Preheat the broiler and line a baking sheet with aluminum foil. In a small bowl, combine ¼ cup of the oil and the garlic. Lightly brush each eggplant slice on both sides with the mixture. Place the slices on the prepared baking sheet and broil until brown, 4 to 5 minutes on each side. Reserve a few slices for garnish. Layer the remaining eggplant slices in the bottom of a Dutch oven. Set aside.

Preheat the oven to 350°.

In a skillet, heat the remaining ¼ cup oil over medium-high heat. Add the chicken and cook, turning occasionally, until golden on all sides, 8 to 10 minutes. Set the chicken pieces on top of the eggplant.

To the oil remaining in the skillet, add the onions, sugar, and spice blend. Cook, stirring occasionally, until the onions are very soft, 10 to 12 minutes. Spoon the onions over the chicken.

In a small bowl, combine the stock, saffron, salt, and pepper. Pour over the onions and cover the dish. Transfer to the oven and bake until the chicken is tender, 40 to 45 minutes. Uncover and bake until the sauce reduces by one-quarter, 15 to 20 minutes. Garnish with the reserved eggplant slices, and serve.

Cornish Hens with Fresh Figs

(Coquelets aux Figues Fraîches)

Serves 4

igs ripen in late summer or early fall. All over Morocco, Sephardic cooks try to incorporate them into their family menus. This luscious tagine, best served with warm crusty bread, is one way of doing so.

8 large onions, thinly sliced
6 tablespoons honey
1 teaspoon salt
½ teaspoon freshly ground black pepper
2 large or 4 small Cornish game hens
2 tablespoons virgin olive oil
12 threads Spanish saffron, toasted and crushed (page 7)
12 fresh figs, peeled and halved

In a heavy ovenproof skillet or Dutch oven, combine the onions with 3 tablespoons of the honey, ½ teaspoon of the salt, and ¼ teaspoon of the pepper. Cook over medium heat, stirring occasionally, until the onions turn a deep caramel color, 25 to 30 minutes.

Meanwhile, wash and dry the hens. In a small bowl, mix the oil with the saffron, the remaining ½ teaspoon salt, and ¼ teaspoon pepper. Coat the hens inside and out with the mixture and set them on top of the onions. Still over medium heat, cover, and cook until the hens are tender and the juices run clear, 45 to 50 minutes.

Preheat the broiler. Remove the hens from the pan and cut them in half, if desired. Return to the pan and surround with the figs. Drizzle the dish with the remaining 3 tablespoons honey. Broil, watching carefully, until the breasts turn brown, 3 to 4 minutes. Transfer to a serving platter and serve.

Meatballs with Swiss Chard

(Boundigaz aux Blettes)

Makes about 34 (1½-inch) meatballs; serves 6 to 8

oundigaz *derives from the Aramaic word for "round object," possibly because of the linguistic influence of Levantine immigrants to the Iberian Peninsula, where today, meatballs are called* albóndigas. *Diminutive balls of ground meat were a signature dish of medieval Spanish Jews, who created clever adaptations, often concealing a whole almond or a piece of cooked egg yolk in their centers.*

Chard

2 (12-ounce) bunches white chard, soaked in water and drained
2 (12-ounce) bunches red chard, soaked in water and drained
2 cups beef or chicken stock (pages 4 and 5)
1 teaspoon ground turmeric
6 threads Spanish saffron, toasted and crushed (page 7)
1 teaspoon salt
3 cloves garlic, minced

Meatballs

1 pound lean ground beef
1 pound ground chicken
1 onion, grated
30 sprigs flat-leaf parsley, chopped
3 eggs, lightly beaten
3 tablespoons water
3 slices crustless white bread, soaked in warm water and squeezed dry
1½ teaspoons ground nutmeg
2 teaspoons salt
¼ teaspoon freshly ground black pepper
2 cups fine semolina or semolina flour
3 to 4 tablespoons olive oil

2 (14-ounce) cans artichoke bottoms, drained
2 tablespoons freshly squeezed lemon juice
Lemon wedges for serving

(continued)

To prepare the chard, trim the leaves from the stem, reserving the stems. Coarsely chop 2 of the leaves. Reserve the remaining leaves for another use. With a vegetable peeler, remove the fibrous outer layer from the stems. Cut each stem down the center lengthwise and then crosswise into 1-inch pieces. In a large skillet, combine the stems, chopped chard leaves, stock, turmeric, saffron, salt, and garlic. Cover and cook over medium heat until the stems are tender, 12 to 15 minutes. Set aside.

To prepare the meatballs, in a large bowl, combine the beef, chicken, onion, parsley, 1 of the eggs, 1 tablespoon of the water, the bread, nutmeg, salt, and pepper. Mix thoroughly. Fashion 1 rounded tablespoon into a ball about 1¼ inches in diameter, wetting your hands frequently to prevent sticking. Repeat until all the meat mixture is used.

Pour the semolina onto a shallow plate. Line another plate with paper towels. In small bowl, beat the remaining 2 eggs with the remaining 2 tablespoons water.

In a large skillet, heat 3 tablespoons of the oil over medium-high heat. Roll the meatballs in the semolina, then in the beaten egg, and once again in the semolina. Set the meatballs in the oil without overcrowding. Cook, turning as needed, until the balls are evenly browned, 6 to 8 minutes. Using a slotted spoon, transfer the meatballs to the paper towels to drain. Proceed in this manner until all the meatballs are browned, adding the remaining tablespoon oil as needed.

Bring the vegetables to a simmer over medium heat. Nestle the meatballs in the chard. Cover and cook until the meatballs are no longer pink in the centers, 20 to 25 minutes. Toss the artichoke bottoms with the lemon juice, add to the dish and heat through. To serve, arrange the artichoke bottoms on a serving platter and place a meatball on each. Mound the chard on the platter, along with the remaining meatballs. Baste with the pan juices and serve with lemon wedges.

Meatballs in Cinnamon-Onion Sauce

(BOUNDIGAZ AUX OIGNONS)

Serves 12

n exotic spice blend elevates prosaic meatballs to a loftier status on the eve of Shabbat. Serve the boundigaz *hot with rice for a light supper, or cold with Dijon mustard or harissa (page 12).*

4 onions
1 pound lean ground beef
2 slices crustless white bread, soaked in warm water and squeezed dry
1 egg, lightly beaten
1 tablespoon "Top of the Shop" Spice Blend (page 23)
1 teaspoon salt
¼ teaspoon freshly ground black pepper
⅔ cup water
½ teaspoon ground cinnamon
2 tablespoons vegetable oil (optional)

Grate 1 of the onions. Slice the remaining 3 onions into ¼-inch slices.

In a large bowl, combine the grated onion, beef, bread, egg, spice blend, salt, and pepper. Mix thoroughly. Shape 1 rounded tablespoon into a ball about 1¼ inches in diameter, wetting your hands frequently to prevent sticking. Repeat until all the meat mixture is used.

In a large saucepan, bring the water to a boil over medium-high heat. Add the meatballs, cover with the sliced onions, and sprinkle with the cinnamon. Decrease the heat to medium. Cook until the meatballs are no longer pink in the centers, 20 to 25 minutes. Add the oil for a richer sauce and serve hot or at room temperature.

Preserved Beef

(KLEEHE)

Serves 12

efore the advent of refrigeration, cooks relied on time-honored methods of preserving beef and lamb. These included dehydration through salting, sun-drying, and extended cooking. The resulting intensely flavored morsels of meat were placed in an earthenware crock, blanketed with a layer of fat, and stored in a cool place in the kitchen. Small portions could be used as needed to prepare hasty yet delicious tagines of seasonal vegetables, or simply savored with a chunk of warm bread. In this recipe, we dispense with the earthenware crock and layer of fat in favor of a modern, frost-free, side-by-side refrigerator.

4 tablespoons vegetable oil
3 pounds boneless chuck roast, cut into ¾-inch cubes (about 6 cups)
½ cup water
1 teaspoon salt
¼ teaspoon freshly ground black pepper

Preheat the oven to 350°.

In a skillet, heat the oil over medium-high heat. Add the meat in batches, without overcrowding, and fry until it is evenly brown on all sides, 15 to 20 minutes. Transfer to an ovenproof dish and add the water, salt, and pepper. Bake until the meat appears desiccated, 1¾ to 2 hours. All the water will have evaporated. Allow to cool and store for up to 1 week in a tightly sealed container in the refrigerator.

Green Beans with Preserved Beef

(Haricots Verts au Kleehe)

Serves 4

reserved beef, called kleehe, *lends its unique flavor to this savory dish of haricots verts. Rice is the perfect accompaniment.*

1 tablespoon virgin olive oil
2 onions, thinly sliced
4 tomatoes, peeled, seeded (page 7), and coarsely chopped
1 garlic clove, minced
1 cup coarsely diced Preserved Beef (page 98)
1 pound green beans (haricots verts preferred), cut into 1-inch pieces
12 pitted green olives, rinsed, drained, and thinly sliced
6 preserved kumquats (page 18),
  rinsed under running water (optional)
1 teaspoon salt
⅛ teaspoon freshly ground black pepper

In a large skillet, heat the oil over medium-high heat. Add the onions and cook, stirring, until they wilt, 4 to 5 minutes. Add the tomatoes, garlic, beef, green beans, olives, and kumquats. Cover and cook until the beans are tender, 10 to 15 minutes. Season with salt and pepper. Continue to cook, uncovered, until the sauce thickens somewhat, 8 to 10 minutes. Serve hot.

Tagine of Beef with Carrots and Turnips

(Tagine de Boeuf aux Carottes et aux Navets)

Serves 4

his popular tagine from Fez will taste even better when prepared a day ahead. A relatively low roasting temperature yields fork-tender beef and buttery-soft root vegetables. Use lamb shoulder instead of beef, if you prefer. Serve with plenty of bread.

3 tablespoons virgin olive oil
1½ pounds boneless beef chuck roast, cut into 1-inch cubes
1 pound carrots, peeled and cut into 3-inch sticks
1 pound small turnips, peeled and quartered
2 onions, quartered
1 teaspoon salt
½ teaspoon freshly ground black pepper
1 teaspoon ground ginger
½ teaspoon ground turmeric
½ cup water
2 tomatoes, peeled, seeded (page 7), and coarsely chopped
10 sprigs cilantro, chopped
4 cloves garlic, minced

Preheat the oven to 350°.

In an ovenproof pan, heat the oil over medium-high heat. Add the meat and cook, turning occasionally, until brown, 5 to 6 minutes. Cover the meat with the carrots, turnips, and onions. In a small bowl, combine the salt, pepper, ginger, and turmeric with the water. Pour over the vegetables. Seal tightly with aluminum foil and bake until the meat is tender, 1½ to 1¾ hours.

Sprinkle the tomatoes, cilantro, and garlic over the vegetables. Continue to bake, uncovered, without disturbing the vegetables, until the tomatoes are cooked, 20 to 30 minutes. Serve hot.

Zahra's Beef with Preserved Kumquats

(Temrika de Boeuf aux Kumquats de Zahra)

Serves 4

he now-abandoned mellah *(Jewish quarter) in the picturesque coastal village of Azemmour was once home to a thriving Sephardic community. There, on the eve of Shabbat, housewives used to deliver their* temrika *(stew) to the neighborhood* ferrane *(public oven), where it would simmer overnight. For a variation, Zahra, Danielle's mother, substitutes lamb shoulder, or even fresh sardines, for the beef. Serve with lots of bread for sopping up the delicious sauce.*

- 2½ pounds bone-in beef chuck roast, cut into 3-inch chunks
- 2 cups water
- 6 red bell peppers, seeded, cored, and cut into 2-inch pieces
- 1 head garlic, separated into cloves and peeled
- ¼ teaspoon ground turmeric
- 1 teaspoon sweet Hungarian paprika
- 12 preserved kumquats (page 18), rinsed under running water and drained
- 10 sprigs cilantro, finely chopped

In a large soup pot, combine the meat and water. Bring to a rolling boil over medium-high heat. Skim off the foam. Decrease the heat to low, cover, and cook until the meat falls off the bone, 2 to 2½ hours. Measure out 1½ cups of the cooking liquid. Set the rest aside for another use.

Place the bell pepper pieces in the bottom of a Dutch oven. Cover with the meat and sprinkle with the garlic cloves. Add the turmeric and paprika to the reserved 1½ cups cooking liquid and pour over the meat. Cover and cook over medium heat until the peppers are soft, 10 to 15 minutes. Nestle the kumquats among the pieces of meat and sprinkle with the cilantro. Decrease the heat to low, cover, and cook until the sauce thickens somewhat, 30 to 35 minutes. Serve hot.

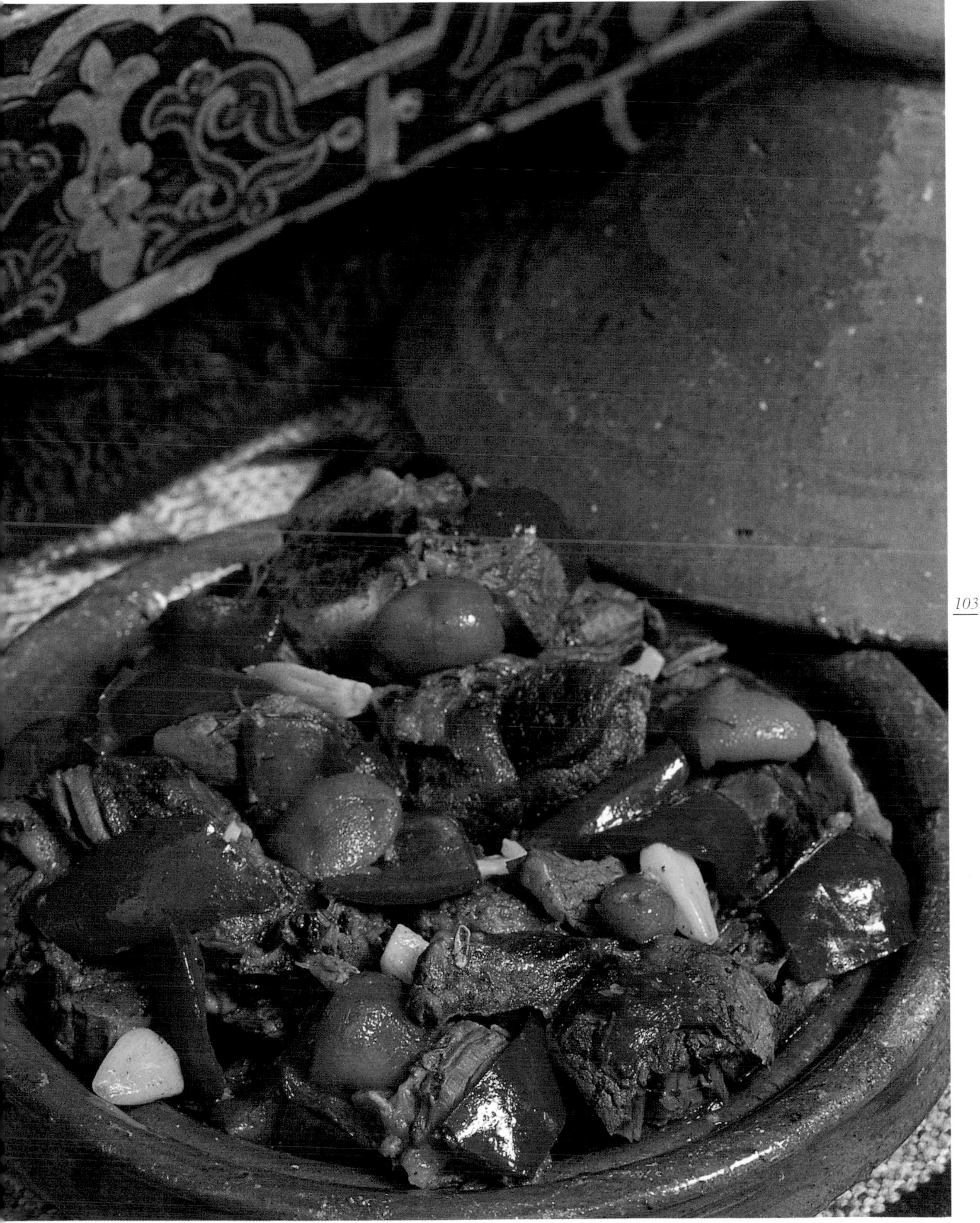

Hanukkah

The eight-day Feast of the Lights, held between the twenty-fifth of Kislev and the second of Tevet, celebrates Judas Maccabeus's victory over Emperor Antiochus IV Epiphanes of Syria and the subsequent rededication of the Temple in Jerusalem, where, miraculously, a one-day supply of oil for the eternal flame lasted eight days. Modern Jews commemorate the event by lighting one compartment of the hanukkiyah *(small hanukkah candelabra) on each of eight consecutive evenings, and by preparing a number of dishes in which olive oil is a prominent ingredient.*

Dinner

FISH DUMPLINGS IN TOMATO SAUCE (PAGE 128)
COUSCOUS WITH VEGETABLES
SEPHARDIC PANCAKES (PAGE 78)
MINT TEA (PAGE 172)

Maman Couriat (née Zahra Aboudarham), mother-in-law of Kitty's great-aunt, Tita, in traditional costume and head scarf, Tétouan, Morocco, circa 1870. (Photo courtesy Scémama family collection.)

Roasted Lamb Shoulder

(EPAULE D'AGNEAU RÔTIE)

Serves 6

anielle departs from tradition by basting the lamb shoulder with a little soy sauce to obtain a richer-looking, more crackly skin. Roasted Potatoes with Chermoula (page 132) and Candied Carrots (page 136) are good choices to accompany the lamb.

1 (3-pound) boneless lamb shoulder, trimmed of fat
1 cup loosely packed flat-leaf parsley, chopped
15 cloves garlic, minced
1½ teaspoons salt
2 teaspoons freshly ground black pepper
¼ cup soy sauce
Lettuce or mint leaves, for serving

Preheat the oven to 400°. Spread the lamb shoulder open on a flat work surface. Sprinkle the parsley, garlic, salt, and pepper down the center of the meat. Fold the sides of the meat over the filling, then the ends, to completely enclose it. Shape the roast into a roll, and tie it with kitchen twine in several places. Place it in a baking pan and baste it with the soy sauce.

Roast until the center registers 140° on a meat thermometer, 20 to 22 minutes per pound for a light pink center. The skin should be crackly and brown.

Let the roast stand for 10 minutes before slicing. Discard the string. Line a serving platter with the lettuce leaves, top with the meat slices, and serve.

Lamb Kebabs

(Brochettes d'Agneau)

Serves 4

oth Muslims and Jews call these grilled kebabs by their French name, brochettes. *Slide the succulent, marinated morsels of tender grilled lamb into a pocket of warm bread, or slip them onto a plate with assorted salads. Serve with saucers of cumin and harissa, for an authentic Moroccan experience.*

2 pounds boneless leg of lamb, trimmed of fat
and cut into 1-inch cubes
15 sprigs cilantro, finely chopped
1 teaspoon sweet Hungarian paprika
2 cloves garlic, minced
½ teaspoon ground cumin, plus additional for dipping
½ teaspoon salt, plus additional for dipping
2 tablespoons freshly squeezed lemon juice
1 tablespoon virgin olive oil
Harissa (page 12), for dipping

In a large bowl, combine the meat with the cilantro, paprika, garlic, ½ teaspoon cumin, ½ teaspoon salt, lemon juice, and olive oil. Cover and refrigerate at least 2 hours, or overnight.

Prepare a fire in a charcoal grill or preheat a gas grill. Thread the meat onto metal skewers, allowing 8 to 10 pieces of meat on each skewer. Place the skewers on the grill rack and grill, turning occasionally, for 5 to 6 minutes for rare.

Serve with little saucers filled with cumin, salt, and harissa, for dipping, on the side.

108

Ground Meat Kebabs

(Kefta)

Serves 4

The smoke that drifted across the grounds of the Vista, California, farmers' market had a familiar fragrance. Kitty followed her nose to a grill operated by a Sephardic vendor from her hometown of Casablanca. Small world! For these kefta, *we use the same distinctive blend of spices he did. Grilling over a charcoal* canoun *(brazier) is the most popular method of cooking. Serve* kefta *hot off the grill as a first course. Accompany with warm bread and individual saucers of ground cumin and harissa for dipping.*

1¼ pounds lean ground beef
½ onion, grated
2 cloves garlic, very finely minced
1 teaspoon ground cumin, plus additional for dipping
1 teaspoon sweet Hungarian paprika
½ teaspoon salt
6 sprigs flat-leaf parsley, finely minced
Harissa (page 12), for dipping (optional)

In a bowl, combine the beef, onion, garlic, cumin, paprika, salt, and parsley. Mix thoroughly until you have a homogeneous mixture. Cover and refrigerate for 1 hour.

Prepare a fire in a charcoal grill, preheat a gas grill, or preheat the broiler. Using your hands, fashion small patties about 2 inches in diameter or pat the meat into a sausage shape around a metal skewer. Wet your hands in between forming each one to prevent sticking.

Grill or broil (on a baking sheet) until done, 4 to 5 minutes on each side for medium rare. Serve immediately, passing the cumin and harissa at the table.

TRUFFLES

Tagine of Lamb with White Truffles

(Tagine d'Agneau aux Terfass)

Serves 6

tagine of lamb and terfass *(truffles) is one of the most anticipated entrées of the Passover Seder. Morocco's Sephardim are especially fond of a unique variety of white truffle called* Terfezia boudieri. *Each spring, east of Rabat, dozens of foragers scour the dense cork oak forest of the Mamora, in search of the precious subterranean tuber. Vendors encase each delicate fungus in ochre-colored clay to prevent desiccation. These they stack in tight, conical mounds along the roadside, to lure passing motorists. Buyers must be on their guard against charlatans, who often substitute potato and other substances for the elusive* terfass. *For sources of canned Moroccan truffles, see page 176.*

- 3 pounds bone-in lamb shoulder, cut into 3-inch pieces
- 8 cloves garlic, minced
- 2 tomatoes, peeled, seeded (page 7), and coarsely chopped
- 2 cups water
- ½ teaspoon salt
- ¼ teaspoon freshly ground black pepper
- 1 (30-ounce) can Moroccan truffles
- 2 tablespoons virgin olive oil

Preheat the oven to 375°. In a Dutch oven, combine the meat, half of the garlic, 1 of the tomatoes, and the water. Cover first with aluminum foil, then with a lid. Bake until the meat is tender, 2 to 2½ hours. Remove from the oven (leaving the heat on) and skim off the fat. Season with salt and pepper.

Meanwhile, drain and rinse the truffles under running water. In a skillet, heat the oil over medium heat. Add the truffles and remaining garlic and cook for 3 to 4 minutes. Add the truffles to the cooked meat along with the remaining tomato. Return to the oven, and continue baking, uncovered, until the truffles are heated through, 10 to 15 minutes.

To serve, transfer the meat to a shallow platter. Surround with the truffles, and spoon the sauce over the dish. Serve hot.

My dear daughters,

I have fond memories of Shabbat eve when you were young. We spent every Friday evening at your grandmother's, until you, Fabienne, were eleven, and Hélène was sixteen. Whether we showed up early or late, Mémé was ready for us, seated demurely in her favorite rocking chair, her long brown hair twisted into an elegant chignon, her shoulders covered in a colorful, fringed shawl. Like a self-assured army general, she took control of her troops.

The aromas of Shabbat and the scent of freshly baked bread welcomed us as we stepped into the hallway of her tidy apartment. All the lights were on, adding to the evening's festive atmosphere. On her crisp, starched tablecloth, Mémé had laid out a dozen of our favorite appetizers, including the pastela of potatoes for which she was famous.

Since your grandfather was no longer with us, it was your father who recited the kiddush, the blessing over the wine, followed by the motze, the special blessing for bread. He broke up a golden loaf into small pieces, which he dipped in salt before distributing to us. After the blessings, Mémé set before us a delicious temrika (stew) redolent of cilantro, or a bowl of tender boundigaz (meatballs) nestled in a bed of onions. She usually prepared an extra side dish just for me, knowing my predilection for her divine carrot preserves. And, of course, she always had a few dozen of your father's favorite cookies for him to take home.

We often returned for the Shabbat meal the following day, sometimes with several unexpected guests in tow, to partake of her memorable dafina (stew). For Mémé, preparations had begun twenty-four hours earlier, on Friday afternoon, at 2 P.M. She combined all the requisite ingredients in a heavy, aluminum Dutch oven. Later that evening, she added the wheat berries, and checked the moisture content. On Saturday morning, a symphony of aromas tempted all who entered her home. But Mémé was adamant: "You must never disturb the dafina while it is cooking!" Sampling had to wait until 1 P.M., when the men returned from the synagogue. A happy chorus of exclamations greeted the nutmeg-scented vapor rising from the serving platter, heaped with tender pieces of meat, mahogany-colored potatoes, glistening caramelized onions, and eggs in cinnamon-tinted shells.

Only after her death, when the duty of preparing the Shabbat meal fell to me, did I fully appreciate your grandmother's labor of love, carrying on family tradition, week after week, with never a word of complaint.

Your loving mother

Shabbat Stew

(Dafina Complète)

Serves 6

Shabbat begins on Friday at sundown and lasts until the first stars appear in the sky on Saturday. During this period, observant Jews must refrain from all work—including culinary activities—in order to concentrate on spiritual matters. A number of rituals define the Shabbat meal served on Saturday upon the men's return from the synagogue.

Dafina, *also called* skhina, *is the traditional dish of Shabbat. The terms derive from the Arabic words* madfoun *(buried) and* skhoon *(hot), respectively. Moroccan Jews employ both terms interchangeably for the traditional stew. In the days when domestic ovens were scarce, housewives carried their* dafina *to the neighborhood* ferrane *(public oven), where it would slow cook until the following afternoon. They paid a laborer from the* ferrane, *called a* tarah *(hard worker), a small fee to safeguard their family's tightly sealed* dafina. *No one dared tamper with the contents of the container entrusted to his care.*

By midday on Saturday, the ferrane *was a beehive of activity, as young people and servants arrived to collect the Shabbat meal. Practical jokes were not uncommon, and occasionally a prankster absconded with a* dafina *belonging to another family. Initial panic gave way to relief when the perpetrator returned with the purloined pot, and a bottle of* mahiya *(fig liquor) to make amends.*

2 (14½-ounce) cans garbanzo beans, drained
2 pounds beef chuck roast or brisket, cut into 2-inch chunks
1 small beef shank bone
1 small beef marrow bone
40 small new potatoes, peeled
2 teaspoons salt
½ teaspoon freshly ground black pepper

Wheat Berries

⅓ cup whole wheat berries (hard wheat preferred), rinsed and drained
1 cup beef stock (page 4)
1 head garlic, papery husk removed
½ teaspoon sweet Hungarian paprika

(continued)

¼ teaspoon salt
1 tablespoon vegetable oil

Rice

1 tablespoon vegetable oil
1 onion, diced
½ cup jasmine rice
1 cup beef stock (page 4)
½ teaspoon salt

Beef Sausage

½ pound ground beef
1 slice crustless white bread, soaked in water and squeezed dry
½ teaspoon salt
¼ teaspoon freshly ground black pepper
½ teaspoon ground ginger
¼ teaspoon ground allspice
⅛ teaspoon ground nutmeg
⅛ teaspoon ground cloves
2 tablespoons rice

6 hard-boiled eggs

Cover the bottom of a large cast-iron roasting pan with the garbanzo beans. (Reserve one of the empty cans.) Top with the beef, shank bone, and marrow bone. Scatter the potatoes around the dish. Season with salt and pepper. Add enough water to just cover the potatoes. Set aside.

To prepare the wheat berries, thoroughly clean the reserved garbanzo bean can. Fill the can with the wheat berries, stock, garlic head, paprika, salt, and vegetable oil. Seal tightly with foil and tie with string. Set aside.

To prepare the rice, in a saucepan, heat the oil over medium-high heat. Add the onion and cook, stirring occasionally, until wilted, 4 to 5 minutes.

(continued)

Add the jasmine rice and cook, stirring, until translucent, 8 to 10 minutes. Add the stock and salt, cover, and decrease the heat to low. Cook until the rice is tender and all the liquid is absorbed, 10 to 12 minutes. Set aside to cool for a few minutes.

Prepare a 10 by 16-inch double layer of aluminum foil. Spoon the rice down the center. Roll up tightly as you would a sausage, sealing the ends. Place on top of the potatoes in the roasting pan.

Preheat the oven to 325°.

To prepare the sausage, in a bowl, combine the ground beef, bread, salt, pepper, ginger, allspice, nutmeg, cloves, and 2 tablespoons rice. Prepare a 10 by 16-inch double layer of aluminum foil. Spoon the meat mixture down the center. Roll up tightly as you would a sausage, sealing the ends. Place on top of the potatoes in the roasting pan.

Nestle the eggs among the other ingredients. Seal the pan tightly, first with foil, then with the lid. Place in the oven and cook until the potatoes are tender, 1½ to 2 hours. Remove from the oven (beware of the steam escaping from the pan). Add a little water if the ingredients appear dried out. Nestle the can of wheat berries among the potatoes. Seal the pan again with the foil and lid and return it to the oven. Continue cooking until all the ingredients, especially the potatoes, acquire a deep caramel color, 4 to 5 hours.

Shell and halve the eggs. Cut the sausage into thick slices. Arrange these and all other components of the *dafina* on separate parts of a large serving platter. Nestle the head of garlic among the wheat berries. Mound the rice on the side of the platter and serve.

Sweet Roasted Vegetables for Rosh Hashanah

(Légumes Sucrés de Rosh Hashanah)

Serves 6

weet roasted vegetables receive a special beraha *(blessing) during Rosh Hashanah. The vegetables symbolize a family's hopes for a new year filled with happiness and prosperity. According to tradition, the various vegetables are kept separate on the serving platter to facilitate their selection as they are blessed.*

1 cup canned garbanzo beans, drained
1 cup plus 2 tablespoons vegetable oil
10 carrots, peeled and cut in half lengthwise
12 leeks, white part only, sliced in half lengthwise
10 small turnips, peeled and quartered
12 boiling onions, peeled
6 zucchini, peeled and cut into 5-inch sticks
2 pounds butternut or winter squash, peeled and cut into 2-inch cubes
5 sticks cinnamon
1 cup raisins
¾ cup sugar
1 teaspoon salt
½ teaspoon freshly ground black pepper
1 cup water

Preheat the oven to 450°. Sprinkle the garbanzos in the bottom of a large roasting pan. Pour the 1 cup oil into a bowl. Add the carrots and toss to coat. With a slotted spoon, transfer the carrots to the roasting pan and set atop the garbanzo beans. Proceed in the same manner with the leeks, turnips, onions, zucchini, and squash, layering the vegetables as you go. Sprinkle the dish with the cinnamon sticks, raisins, sugar, salt, pepper, and water.

Roast until the vegetables turn light brown, 15 to 20 minutes. Decrease the oven temperature to 350°. Continue to roast until the vegetables are tender and caramelized, 1¼ to 1½ hours. Add the 2 tablespoons oil, if necessary, to prevent the vegetables from drying out. Serve hot.

Oriza of Wheat Berries and Sweet Potatoes

(Oriza aux Patates Douces de Marisa)

Serves 4

he word "oriza" derives from "harissa," a recipe for which is found in Manuscrito Anónimo, a thirteenth-century Andalusian cookbook. At that time, harissa (not to be confused with the more modern hot sauce of the same name on page 12) was a celebrated nutritious porridge of soaked wheat berries, garbanzo beans, pounded meat, melted mutton fat, and cinnamon. Sephardic cooks transformed harissa into this meatless adaptation, called oriza. The baked garlic loses most of its pungency through the lengthy cooking process and attains the consistency of soft butter—perfect for spreading on a chunk of warm, crusty bread.

2 tablespoons virgin olive oil
2 onions, finely diced
1 teaspoon sweet Hungarian paprika
¾ cup whole wheat berries, rinsed and drained
2 cups water
1 teaspoon salt
1 small sweet potato or yam, peeled and cut into ½-inch cubes
2 heads garlic, papery husk removed

Preheat the oven to 325°.

In a heavy ovenproof skillet or Dutch oven, heat the olive oil over medium-high heat. Add the onions and paprika and cook, stirring occasionally, until the onions are soft, 6 to 8 minutes. Add the wheat berries and stir to coat for 2 to 3 minutes. Add the water, salt, sweet potato, and garlic. Seal the pan tightly with aluminum foil and then with a lid.

Bake until the wheat berries are tender but still a little chewy, 2½ to 3 hours. Serve immediately with the garlic on the side.

Couscous with Onion and Raisin Confit

(Couscous de la Mimouna)

Serves 8

The fragrance of orange blossom and cinnamon permeates the couscous prepared for the feast of La Mimouna, on the last evening of Passover. Traditionally, families in the mellah *threw open their doors to welcome Jewish and Muslim friends alike.*

8 cups beef stock (page 4)
5 tablespoons vegetable oil
1 cup whole blanched almonds
½ pound onions
¼ cup granulated sugar
2 teaspoons ground cinnamon, plus additional for garnish
2 teaspoons salt
4 ounces (about ¾ cup) seedless raisins, plumped in warm water and drained
2 cups couscous
1 to 2 tablespoons orange blossom water (page 6)
Confectioners' sugar, for serving

Bring the stock to a boil in a stockpot until reduced by one-quarter. Set aside.

In a large skillet, heat 2 tablespoons of the oil over medium heat. Add the almonds and fry, shaking the pan occasionally, until light gold, 2 to 3 minutes. Using a slotted spoon, transfer to a bowl and set aside.

Slice the onions and add them to the same skillet with 1 tablespoon of the oil and 2 tablespoons of the stock. Cover and cook until the onions are soft, 10 to 15 minutes. Add the granulated sugar, cinnamon, and 1 teaspoon of the salt. Decrease the heat to medium-low, partially cover, and continue to cook, stirring occasionally, until the onions acquire a deep caramel color, 1¼ to 1½ hours. Add the raisins and heat through, 2 to 3 minutes.

Meanwhile, prepare the couscous. In a saucepan, combine 2⅔ cups of the

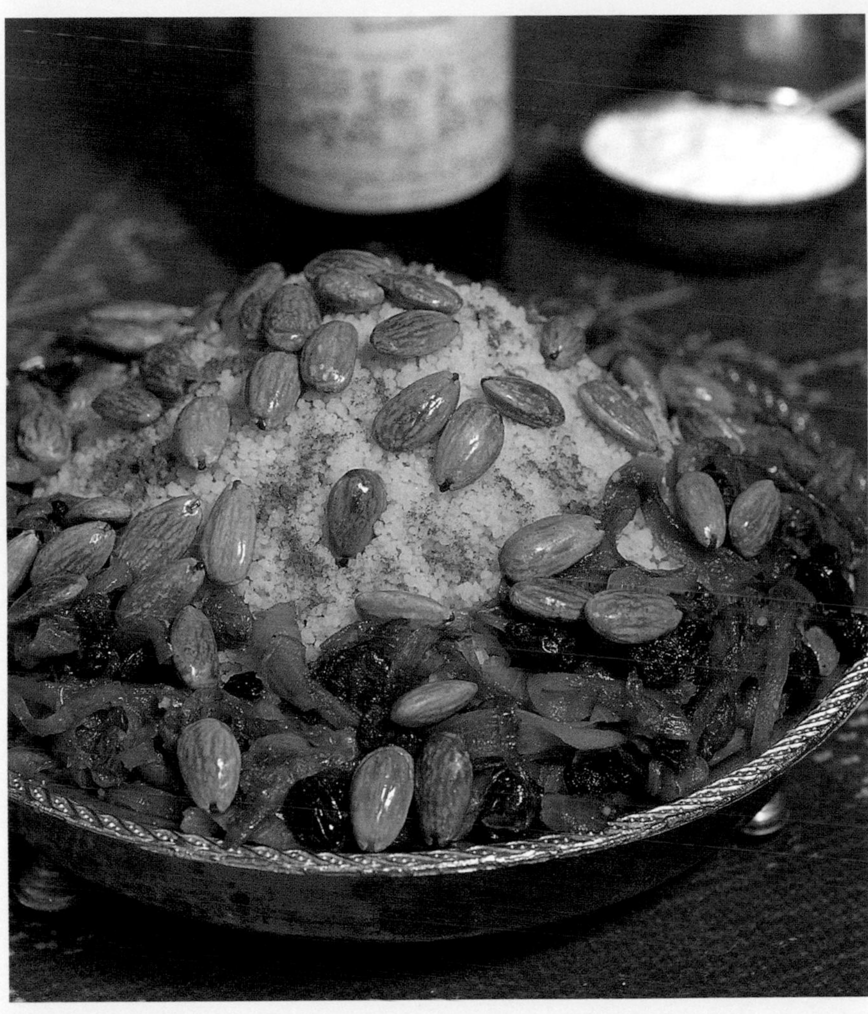

stock, the remaining 2 tablespoons oil, and the remaining 1 teaspoon salt and bring to a boil. Remove from the heat. Add the couscous in a stream, stir once, cover, and set aside until the couscous is tender and the stock is absorbed, 12 to 15 minutes.

Reheat the remaining beef stock. Combine ½ cup of the heated stock with the orange blossom water to taste and mix with the couscous.

Mound the couscous on a warm serving platter. Spoon the onion mixture around the base. Sprinkle with cinnamon and garnish with the fried almonds. Serve with the confectioners' sugar and remaining stock on the side.

Turkey Couscous for Yom Kippur

(Couscous à la Dinde de Yom Kippur)

Serves 8

ouscous topped with sweetened, caramelized vegetables and dusted with cinnamon was the signature dish of Morocco's Sephardic Jews. It wasn't until the mid-1950s that they followed the lead of Algerian Sephardim and Moroccan Muslims, to adopt a savory couscous.

4 tablespoons virgin olive oil
2 onions, quartered
3 turkey legs (about 3½ pounds)
1 (14¼-ounce) can whole tomatoes, undrained
15 sprigs cilantro, tied together with kitchen twine
10⅔ cups water
1 teaspoon ground turmeric
2 teaspoons ground ginger
4 carrots, peeled and cut into 3-inch sticks
4 turnips, peeled and quartered
1 pound pumpkin or winter squash, peeled and cut into 2-inch chunks
1 small cabbage, quartered
2 tablespoons salt
1 teaspoon freshly ground black pepper
½ cup canned garbanzo beans, drained
2 cups couscous
¼ cup raisins, plumped in warm water and drained
Confectioners' sugar
2 tablespoons harissa (page 12; optional)

In a *couscoussier* or a large soup pot over medium-high heat, heat 2 tablespoons of the olive oil. Add the onions and cook until soft, 4 to 5 minutes. Add the turkey and cook, stirring occasionally, until golden, 5 to 6 minutes. Add the tomatoes, cilantro, and 8 cups of the water. Bring to a rolling boil, cover, and cook for 10 to 15 minutes. Decrease the heat to medium and add the turmeric, ginger, carrots, and turnips. Cover and cook until the carrots are tender, 20 to 25 minutes.

Preheat the oven to 200°. With a slotted spoon, transfer the vegetables to an ovenproof dish and place them in the oven to keep warm. Add the pumpkin and the cabbage to the pot. Cook, covered, until the pumpkin is tender, 15 to 20 minutes. With a slotted spoon, add the vegetables to the pan in the oven. Discard the cilantro. Add 4 teaspoons of the salt, the pepper, and garbanzos to the pot. Keep it simmering until you are ready to serve.

Meanwhile, prepare the couscous. In a saucepan, combine the remaining 2⅔ cups water, the remaining 2 tablespoons olive oil, and the remaining 2 teaspoons salt and bring to a boil. Remove from the heat. Add the couscous and the raisins in a stream. Stir once, cover, and set aside until the couscous is tender, 12 to 15 minutes.

Fluff the couscous with a fork and mound it on a large serving platter. Top with the cooked vegetables and turkey legs. Remove the garbanzo beans from the pot with a slotted spoon. Sprinkle the beans over the platter and dust with sugar. In a small bowl, mix 1 cup of the cooking liquid with the harissa. Serve on the side, along with another bowl filled with the remaining cooking liquid.

Thursday Evening's Buttered Couscous

(Couscous au Beurre du Jeudi Soir)

Serves 6

hursday was a busy day for Sephardic cooks. Cleaning house and preparing a variety of cooked salads for Shabbat left barely enough time to put together the evening meal. For this reason, dinner usually consisted of a simple, yet nourishing, buttered couscous accompanied by a glass of mint tea.

2⅔ cups water
1 teaspoon salt
4 tablespoons unsalted butter
2 cups couscous
2 to 3 tablespoons sugar
1 cup milk, warmed
¼ cup raisins, plumped in warm water and drained

In a saucepan, combine the water, salt, and 2 tablespoons of the butter and bring to a boil. Remove from the heat. Add the couscous in a stream. Stir once, cover, and set aside until the couscous is tender, 12 to 15 minutes.

Add the remaining 2 tablespoons butter and the sugar to the couscous and fluff with a fork. Mound the couscous on a serving platter. Pour the warm milk over the dish. Sprinkle with the raisins and serve hot.

My darling daughter,

You have asked me how we used to celebrate Hanukkah in Fez. It was a festive winter celebration when the whole family gathered around the hanukkiyah (oil-burning lamp) at sundown.

Uncle David called for everyone to gather around in a loud, booming voice. He would then ceremoniously light the appropriate number of hemp wicks, which his mother, Gracia, handmade for the occasion. Uncle David's children recited the lovely Hanukkah prayer, while my brother and I listened, entranced by the mellifluous sounds of the Hebrew words. I remember the acrid smell of the olive oil burning in the lamps and the long, smoky trail the oil left on the wall.

After the prayer, we would attack the pyramid of Aunt Judith's powdered beignets de hanoukka (doughnuts) set in the center of the dining room table. How we laughed at the sight of the white mustaches of confectioners' sugar we all wore! On other nights, we were invited to grandmother Esther's, or to your Aunt Sultana's, for a delectable meat and vegetable couscous, the perfect meal for a chilly December evening. As custom warranted, their couscous was liberally sprinkled with confectioners' sugar and cinnamon.

I'm saving an antique bronze hanukkiyah for you. It belonged to your grandmother. Treasure it, as I have, for oil lamps such as these are becoming quite rare. With it, my darling, I hope you and your sister will perpetuate our traditions. Light your hanukkiyah to brighten up your home, and gather your friends around you. You are always in our thoughts.

Happy holidays!

Your loving mother

Fresh Sardine "Sandwiches"

(SARDINES MZOUWEJJ)

Serves 6

n Essaouira, the quaint seaport village along Morocco's Atlantic coast, townspeople await the return of the fishing fleet. Workers spring into action as soon as the boats dock, anxious to unload the precious cargo. Within minutes, fish peddlers fan out through the narrow streets of the ancient medina with the day's catch. Housewives examine the contents of the heavy straw baskets before selecting the finest of the fresh, silvery sardines lying beneath a glistening blanket of wet seaweed. These delectable "sandwiches" are as popular at the Sephardic table as they are with the Muslim patrons who surround the fast food kiosks in the Essaouira's open-air market. In the United States, fresh sardines are commonly sold in Asian markets.

12 large, fresh sardines
15 sprigs cilantro, minced
½ teaspoon ground cumin
2 cloves garlic, minced
Juice of 2 lemons
2 tablespoons extra virgin olive oil
Vegetable oil, for frying
1 cup all-purpose flour
1 egg, lightly beaten
2 teaspoons sweet Hungarian paprika
Wedges of lemon, for serving

Scale the fish under cold running water. Cut off the heads. With kitchen shears, slit open the belly of each sardine and discard the innards. Using your fingers, gently pull the spine away from the flesh, leaving the skin and tail intact. Trim the edges, and discard the bones. Rinse well under running water. Set in a colander to drain.

In a shallow dish large enough to accommodate the sardines in one layer, combine the cilantro, cumin, garlic, juice from 1 of the lemons, and the olive oil. Coat each sardine on both sides with the mixture. Cover and refrigerate for 2 to 24 hours.

Pour the vegetable oil into a large skillet to a depth of 1 inch. Bring to the smoking point over medium heat. Meanwhile, place the flour in a shallow dish and the egg in another. Press 2 sardines together, skin sides out, to form a "sandwich." Coat first with flour, then dip in the beaten egg, and coat again with flour. Holding the "sandwich" by the tail, gently set it in the hot oil. Continue with the remaining fish. Fry until golden, 5 to 6 minutes on each side. With a spatula, transfer to paper towels to drain.

In a small bowl, combine the juice of the remaining lemon with the paprika. Layer the fried sardines in a shallow serving dish. Cover with the lemon-paprika sauce. Serve hot or at room temperature with lemon wedges. The sardines will keep for up to 4 days in an airtight container in the refrigerator.

Fish Dumplings in Tomato Sauce

(Quenelles de Poisson à la Sauce Tomate)

Makes about 30; serves 6

ephardic cooks use strong-flavored inexpensive fish, such as mackerel or sardines, to make these airy dumplings. Here, we substitute milder fillets of red snapper or halibut. Add several tablespoons of olive oil to the pan just before serving to give the sauce extra body and sheen. Serve with plenty of crusty bread.

Dumplings

2 pounds boneless fish fillets such as red snapper or halibut
5 cloves garlic, minced
10 sprigs cilantro, finely chopped
1 egg, lightly beaten
1 teaspoon salt
¼ teaspoon freshly ground black pepper

3 cups water
4 tomatoes, peeled, seeded (page 7), and coarsely chopped
3 cloves garlic, minced
5 sprigs cilantro, minced
¾ teaspoon salt
2 tablespoons capers, drained
3 tablespoons virgin olive oil

To prepare the dumplings, in a food processor, combine the fish, garlic, cilantro, egg, salt, and pepper and process until smooth. Transfer to a bowl, cover, and refrigerate for 30 minutes.

In a large saucepan, bring the water to a steady simmer. Wet your hands to prevent sticking. Using 1 rounded tablespoon, fashion the ground fish into tapered dumplings about 2 inches long and 1¼ inches in diameter. Drop gently into the simmering water. Continue in this manner, wetting your hands in between forming each one, until all the fish mixture is used.

Cover the quenelles with the tomatoes, garlic, cilantro, and salt. Increase the heat to medium. Cook, uncovered, until the sauce thickens somewhat, 15 to 20 minutes. Five minutes before serving time, add the capers and the olive oil.

Transfer the quenelles and the sauce to a shallow bowl. Serve hot.

Fish Fillets Fez Style

(Poisson à la Fassi)

Serves 6

Seafood fillets are a frequent first course during the new year celebrations of Rosh Hashanah. A variation of the recipe substitutes preserved kumquats for the lemon slices.

1 tablespoon salt
2 lemons, cut into ¼-inch slices, or 8 preserved kumquats (page 18), rinsed under running water
4 potatoes, peeled and cut into ¼-inch slices
6 (6-ounce) boned fish fillets (snapper, halibut, or orange roughy), patted dry
4 tomatoes, cut into ¼-inch slices
½ teaspoon ground turmeric
1 cup water
10 sprigs flat-leaf parsley, finely chopped
6 cloves garlic, minced
¼ teaspoon freshly ground black pepper
3 tablespoons virgin olive oil (optional)

Lightly salt the lemon slices on both sides. (Omit the salt if using preserved kumquats.) Set aside.

Place the potatoes in the bottom of a Dutch oven or ovenproof casserole. Cover with the fish fillets and tomatoes. Add the turmeric and water. Cover and cook over medium heat until the potatoes are partially tender, 10 to 12 minutes. Add a layer of lemon slices and sprinkle with the parsley, garlic, and pepper. Cover and cook until the fish is flaky, 18 to 20 minutes. Spoon the olive oil over the dish and serve hot.

Fish Fillets with Garbanzo Beans

(Temrika del' Hemms)

Serves 12

he Jews of Fez and the neighboring town of Sefrou, Morocco's cherry capital, prepare this temrika *(stew) on the eve of Shabbat.*

2 cups water
1 head garlic, separated into cloves and peeled
2 mild dried chiles, seeded, soaked, and coarsely chopped
1 teaspoon ground turmeric
1 teaspoon sweet Hungarian paprika
1 (14¼-ounce) can garbanzo beans, drained
1 teaspoon salt
4 (6-ounce) boned fish fillets (snapper, halibut, or orange roughy), patted dry
15 sprigs cilantro, minced

In a small Dutch oven over medium-high heat, combine the water, garlic, chiles, turmeric, and paprika and bring to a boil. Add the garbanzo beans and salt and stir to blend. Decrease the heat to medium. Set the fish on top of the garbanzos and sprinkle with the cilantro. Partially cover and cook until the fish fillets are firm and no longer translucent, 20 to 25 minutes. Serve immediately.

Roasted Potatoes with Chermoula

(Pommes de Terre Rôties à la Chermoula)

Serves 12

hermoula, the quintessential Moroccan spice blend, is gaining favor among America's top chefs. Clever creators of fusion recipes have discovered what Moroccan cooks have known for centuries—that the distinctive and versatile chermoula marries as well with beef and lamb as it does with fish or vegetables, like the roasted potatoes in this simple, yet delicious recipe. Many Sephardic cooks steam the potatoes in a colander-like keskes *before marinating and roasting, to ensure a soft center within a well-cooked, reddish-gold exterior. In this variation, we add several threads of Spanish saffron to the classic chermoula blend.*

2 pounds potatoes, peeled and cut into ½-inch wedges
1¾ teaspoons salt
3 tablespoons virgin olive oil
1 teaspoon sweet Hungarian paprika
1½ teaspoons ground cumin
5 threads Spanish saffron, toasted and crushed (page 7)
3 cloves garlic, minced

Fill the bottom part of a *couscoussier* or large soup pot with water and bring to a boil over high heat. Place the potatoes in a colander that fits tightly over the soup pot. Steam until partially tender, 10 to 15 minutes. Set aside to partially cool. Preheat the oven to 425°.

In a bowl, combine the potatoes with the salt, oil, paprika, cumin, saffron, and garlic. Set the wedges in a baking dish large enough to accommodate them in one layer, or on a foil-lined baking sheet. Roast, turning over once or twice, until golden orange-brown, 35 to 40 minutes. Serve hot.

Potato Stew

(Temrika de Patata)

Serves 4

ephardic families of Tangier, a cosmopolitan city on Morocco's Mediterranean coast, savor this simple yet satisfying dish on the eve of Passover. They often incorporate morsels of preserved beef called kleehe.

2 tablespoons virgin olive oil
2 onions, finely diced
1½ pounds potatoes, cut into ¼-inch slices
4 cloves garlic, peeled and thinly sliced
1 cup Preserved Beef (page 98)
1 teaspoon dried oregano, crushed
¼ teaspoon dried thyme
1 teaspoon salt
¼ teaspoon freshly ground black pepper
⅓ cup water
2 tablespoons white vinegar

In a large skillet, heat the oil over medium-high heat. Add the onions and cook, stirring occasionally, until golden, 4 to 5 minutes. Cover with one-third of the potato slices. Scatter half of the garlic and half of the beef over the potatoes. In a small bowl, combine the oregano, thyme, salt, and pepper. Sprinkle half of the herb mixture over the beef. Scatter the remaining garlic and beef. Top with another layer of potatoes and the remaining herb mixture. Add the water, cover tightly, and decrease the heat to medium. Cook until the potatoes are tender, 20 to 25 minutes. Sprinkle the dish with vinegar. Heat through for 2 to 3 minutes, and serve.

Winter Squash with Caramelized Onions

(Cassolita)

Serves 4

innamon-scented caramelized onions and fried almonds crown this dish of baked squash that traditionally complements the couscous of Tétouan, a city steeped in Andalusian culture and cuisine. In Kitty's family, cassolita *or* cazuelita *(little pot) always accompanies a platter of couscous. She serves it with her Thanksgiving turkey as well.*

2 pounds winter squash, peeled, seeded, and cut into 2-inch pieces
3 tablespoons vegetable oil
¼ cup (about 1 ounce) slivered almonds
3 large onions, thinly sliced
¼ cup sugar
2 teaspoons ground cinnamon
½ cup raisins, plumped in warm water and drained
Salt and freshly ground black pepper

Preheat the oven to 375°. Place the squash in an ovenproof dish and bake until tender, 50 to 60 minutes.

Meanwhile, in a skillet, heat the oil over medium-high heat. Add the almonds and fry until golden, 3 to 4 minutes. With a slotted spoon, transfer the nuts to paper towels to drain.

Add the onions to the oil in the skillet. Cook, stirring occasionally, until soft, 8 to 10 minutes. Add the sugar and cinnamon, decrease the heat to medium, and continue cooking until the onions turn brown, 20 to 25 minutes. Add the raisins and season to taste with salt and pepper. Cook, stirring, until heated through. Transfer the squash to a warm serving platter. Spread the onion mixture evenly over the squash, sprinkle with the fried almonds, and serve.

Candied Carrots

(Carottes Confites)

Serves 8

ustrous candied carrots make a wonderful accompaniment for a succulent lamb shoulder or juicy roasted chicken. Cook them over steady, low heat to ensure an even, translucent glaze.

2 pounds peeled baby carrots
¼ cup plus 2 tablespoons sugar
3 tablespoons vegetable oil
Juice of ½ lemon

In a large saucepan filled with boiling water, cook the carrots until tender, 12 to 15 minutes. Drain and return to the pan. Add the sugar, oil, and lemon juice. Partially cover and cook over low heat, stirring gently once or twice so as not to damage the carrots, until evenly glazed, 1¼ to 1½ hours. Serve hot.

Figs in Orange Juice

(Figues au Jus d'Orange)

Serves 6

igs are one of the most frequently mentioned fruits in the Holy Scriptures, and the fig tree is the first plant given by name in the Book of Genesis. The biblical verse, Micah 4:4 ". . . sit everyman under his vine and under his fig tree: and none shall make them afraid . . ." connects the bucolic image of fig boughs with peace and prosperity. For this reason, the fruit holds an honored place at the Sephardic table during the midwinter feast of Tu B'Shevat, the Jewish New Year for the Trees. On this day, the ritual meal features various fresh and dried fruit. In this recipe, we combine dried apricots with the figs for a more colorful dish.

1 pound whole dried Mission figs, rinsed under running water
½ cup dried apricots
Juice of 2 oranges
¼ teaspoon salt
¼ teaspoon freshly ground black pepper
2 tablespoons vegetable oil

In a bowl, combine the figs and apricots with 2 cups of warm water. Soak for 30 minutes and drain.

In a saucepan, combine the figs, apricots, orange juice, salt, and pepper over medium heat. Cook, covered, until the figs are plump and tender, 15 to 20 minutes. Add the oil and continue to cook until the sauce reduces by one-quarter. Serve hot or at room temperature as a side dish.

Savory Wedding Flan

(T'Faya)

Serves 6

ustom dictates that newlywed Sephardic couples open their wedding presents in front of assembled family and friends, who delight in proffering extemporaneous comments as to each gift's merits, suitability, or appearance, while speculating on its monetary value. As part of the post-nuptial celebrations, the bride and groom feast on generous helpings of light, nutritious t'faya.

2 tablespoons virgin olive oil
½ pound chicken livers
3 eggs, lightly beaten
2 cups chicken stock (page 5)
¼ teaspoon salt
¼ teaspoon freshly ground black pepper

In a small skillet, heat the olive oil over medium-high heat. Add the livers and cook, turning occasionally, until no longer pink, 8 to 10 minutes. Remove from the pan and cut into a ¼-inch dice.

Preheat the oven to 425°. Lightly oil a 1-quart ovenproof bowl.

In a separate large bowl, whisk the eggs with the stock until frothy. Season with the salt and pepper and add the livers. Pour the mixture into the prepared bowl. Set the bowl into a larger baking dish. Pour water halfway up the sides of the bowl.

Bake until the *t'faya* sets and a knife inserted in the center comes out clean, 18 to 20 minutes. Alternatively, the flan can be microwaved in a microwave-proof bowl. Set the temperature to high and microwave until set, 8 to 10 minutes, rotating the bowl every 2 minutes. Serve warm directly from the bowl.

Zahra and Jacob Aflalo, Danielle's parents, on their wedding day, Fez, July 3, 1944.
(Photo courtesy Aflalo-Mamane family collection.)

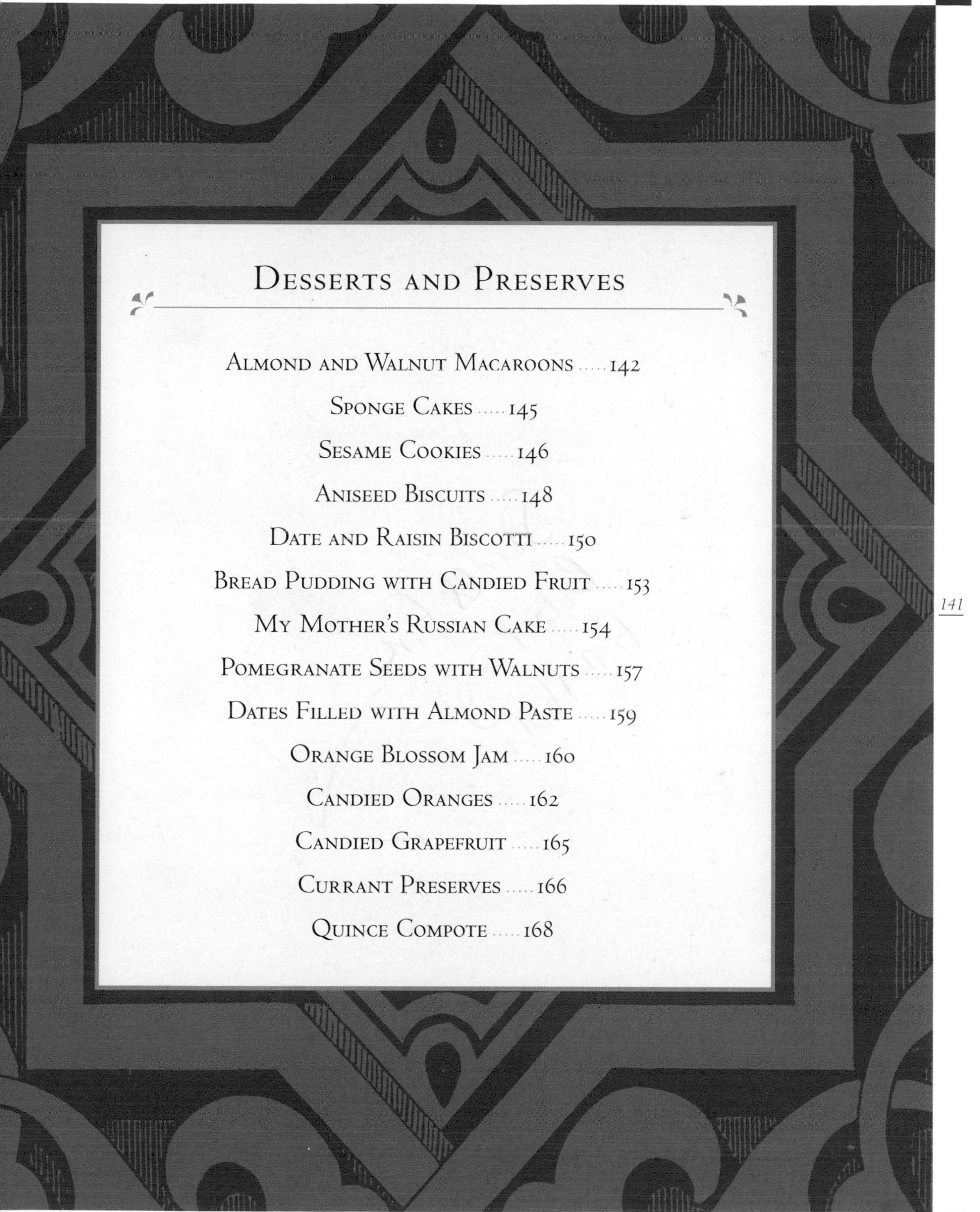

Desserts and Preserves

Almond and Walnut Macaroons 142

Sponge Cakes 145

Sesame Cookies 146

Aniseed Biscuits 148

Date and Raisin Biscotti 150

Bread Pudding with Candied Fruit 153

My Mother's Russian Cake 154

Pomegranate Seeds with Walnuts 157

Dates Filled with Almond Paste 159

Orange Blossom Jam 160

Candied Oranges 162

Candied Grapefruit 165

Currant Preserves 166

Quince Compote 168

Almond and Walnut Macaroons

(Truffes aux Amandes et aux Noix)

Makes about 30

ince these meringue-like macaroons contain no dairy products, they can be served at the conclusion of any meal, even those featuring meat dishes.

2 cups almond meal (about 12 ounces whole almonds ground to a powder)
1 cup walnut meal (about 6 ounces walnut halves ground to a powder)
1½ cups sifted confectioners' sugar
3 large egg whites
1 teaspoon vanilla extract

Preheat the oven to 325°. Place 35 (1½-inch) fluted paper cups on a baking sheet.

In a large bowl, mix together the almond meal, walnut meal, and 1 cup of the sugar. Sprinkle the remaining sugar on a large plate.

In a large bowl, using an electric mixer on high speed, beat the egg whites and vanilla until stiff peaks form. Using a spatula, gently fold the nut mixture into the egg whites. With your fingers, knead lightly to obtain a homogeneous dough.

In between the palms of your hands, fashion balls 1 inch in diameter. Roll each ball in the sugar and set it inside a paper cup.

Bake until the macaroons turn light gold, 20 to 25 minutes. Remove from the oven and let cool. Store in a tightly sealed container for up to 2 weeks.

Tisha B'Av

A day of fasting commemorates the destruction of the First and the Second Temples. Many Moroccan Jews use the occasion to remember the Sephardic exile at the time of the Spanish Inquisition. Sephardim break the fast with a variety of legume-based dishes.

Dinner

Lentil and Garbanzo Bean Soup (page 46)
Chicken with Onions and Tomatoes (page 87)
Fresh, seasonal fruit
Assorted pastries and Mint Tea (page 172)

Sephardic women on their way to participate in a *visita*, Debdou, Morocco, circa 1900. (Photo courtesy Jacques Mamane. Gift to Diaspora Museum, Tel Aviv, Israel.)

Sponge Cakes

(Pallébés)

Makes about 16

he name pallébé *comes from the French* pain levé *(risen bread). It is the most traditional of all Sephardic cakes, and the foundation for numerous other desserts and petits fours. In days gone by, hostesses made individual-sized* pallébés *for a* visita *(page 34). Saucers of candied oranges, candied grapefruit, and orange blossom jam accompanied the small cakes. Guests were free to assemble customized desserts by sandwiching the homemade preserves between two warm, round* pallébés. *A solicitous hostess always made more cakes than she needed, so her guests, especially those of more modest means, would have some to take home to their families.*

¾ cup all-purpose flour
⅛ teaspoon salt
½ teaspoon baking powder
3 large eggs, separated
¼ cup sugar
3 tablespoons vegetable oil

Preheat the oven to 350°.

In a large bowl, mix together the flour, salt, and baking powder.

In a separate bowl, using an electric mixer on high speed, beat the egg whites until stiff peaks form.

In another bowl, using the mixer on medium speed, beat the sugar with the egg yolks and oil until the mixture turns a pale yellow. In batches, gently fold in the flour and the egg whites, blending thoroughly after each addition. Using rounded tablespoons, drop the batter onto a nonstick baking sheet.

Bake until golden and lightly browned around the edges, 12 to 15 minutes. Remove from the oven and let cool. *Pallébés* taste best on the day they are made. Store any leftovers in an airtight container at room temperature.

Sesame Cookies

(Biscuits au Sésame)

Makes about 15

he ancient Egyptians, Babylonians, and Greeks all cultivated sesame seeds and included them in their diet. For Sephardic Jews, they symbolize prosperity for the new year celebrations of Rosh Hashanah.

1½ cups all-purpose flour
1 teaspoon baking powder
½ cup plus 2 tablespoons vegetable oil
½ cup unhulled sesame seeds, toasted (page 8)
½ cup confectioners' sugar
1 teaspoon vanilla extract
2 tablespoons cold water
Cinnamon, for sprinkling

Preheat the oven to 375°.

In a bowl, combine the flour and baking powder. In another bowl, combine the oil, sesame seeds, sugar, and vanilla. Add the flour mixture and water in increments, mixing with your fingers until you have a dough that resembles very coarse crumbs.

Using 2 tablespoons of the dough, fashion rounded patties about 2 inches in diameter. Set them on a baking sheet and flatten lightly with the tips of your fingers. Sprinkle each one with a little cinnamon.

Bake until light gold, 20 to 22 minutes. Remove from the oven and let cool on the baking sheet for 5 to 10 minutes. Using a spatula, transfer to a wire rack. The cookies will harden somewhat. Store in an airtight container for up to 2 weeks.

Aniseed Biscuits

(Galettes à l'Anis)

Makes about 35

others keep plenty of these lightly sweetened galettes on hand for between-meal treats. For variation, they shape the dough into rings. The use of a pasta machine greatly facilitates the task of rolling the dough to a uniform thickness. Substitute cumin seed for anise, if you prefer.

2⅓ cups all-purpose flour, plus additional for dusting
I teaspoon baking powder
I teaspoon salt
I tablespoon aniseeds, toasted (page 8)
I tablespoon sesame seeds, toasted (page 8)
⅓ cup plus I tablespoon sugar
¼ cup vegetable oil
I egg, lightly beaten
½ cup warm water

Preheat the oven to 350°.

In a bowl, combine the flour, baking powder, salt, aniseeds, and sesame seeds.

In a large bowl, using an electric mixer on medium speed, combine the sugar, oil, and egg. Beat until blended and pale yellow. Fold in the flour mixture and add the water in increments, mixing to make a soft dough.

Transfer the dough to a lightly floured work surface and knead for 2 or 3 minutes. Divide the dough into 3 equal portions.

If using a pasta machine, set the smooth lasagna roller to its widest opening. Pass I portion of the dough through the rollers. Dust the strip of dough lightly with flour. Fold it over three times and roll it through the pasta machine again. Repeat the folding and rolling process two more times. The dough should be about 3⁄16-inch thick. Repeat with the remaining 2 portions of dough. Transfer the sheets to a lightly floured work surface.

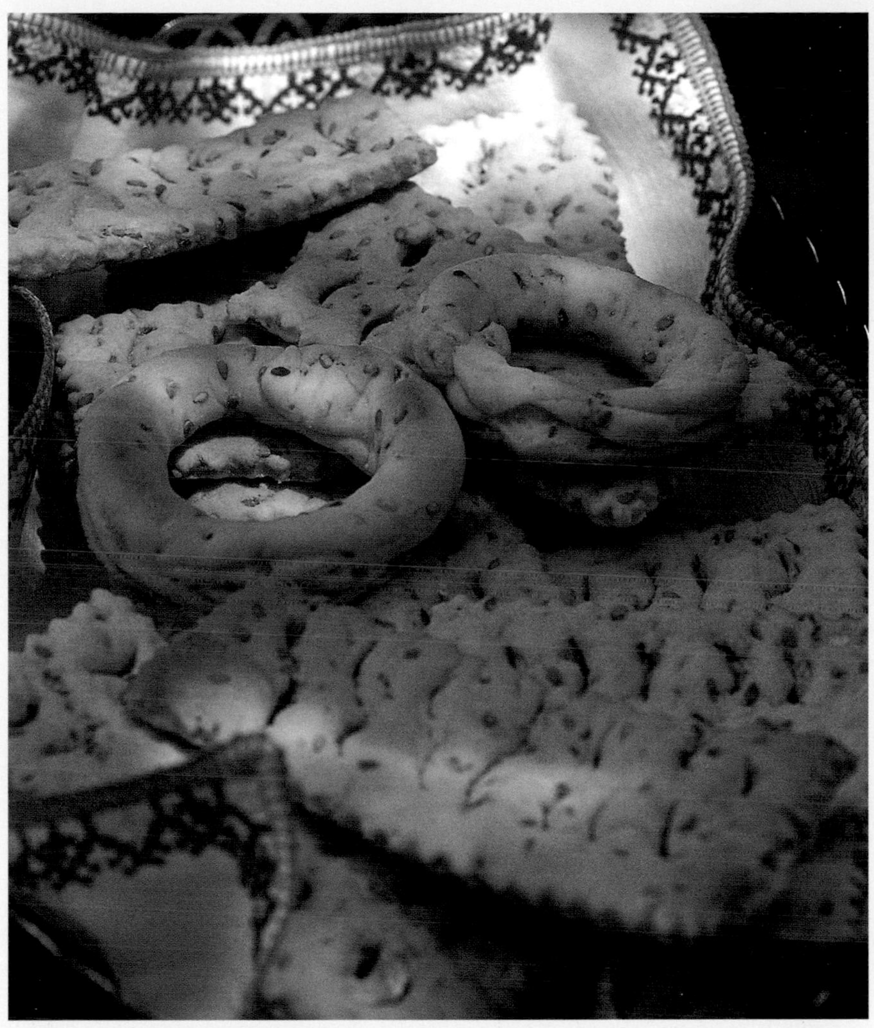

If rolling by hand, lightly flour the work surface and roll 1 portion of the dough out to a 9 by 9-inch square. Repeat with the 2 remaining portions of dough. Cut each square into 2 equal rectangles.

Using a pastry crimper, cut each strip into 4½ by 1½-inch rectangles. With the tines of a fork, make holes down the length of each galette. Transfer to a nonstick baking sheet.

Bake until the galettes turn a light gold, 18 to 20 minutes. Cool on a rack. Store in a tightly sealed container for up to 1 week.

Date and Raisin Biscotti

(Croquets)

Makes about 34

n assortment of delicately sweetened biscotti and a steaming cup of café au lait is continental breakfast, Fassi style. These crumbly biscotti will reappear around five o'clock when children return from school, or friends drop by for a glass of fragrant mint tea.

½ cup raisins
¼ cup chopped dates
¼ cup white rum
2¼ cups all-purpose flour
1 teaspoon baking powder
½ teaspoon salt
4 eggs
⅓ cup vegetable oil
½ cup plus 2 tablespoons sugar
½ cup walnut or pecan pieces
1 teaspoon water

Preheat the oven to 350°. Line a baking sheet with aluminum foil and lightly grease the foil.

In a small bowl, soak the raisins and dates in the rum until plumped, 15 to 20 minutes. Drain and set aside.

In a large bowl, combine the flour, baking powder, and salt.

In the bowl of a stand mixer, beat 3 of the eggs on medium speed until they turn pale yellow. Add the oil and sugar in batches, and beat until dissolved. Remove the bowl from the mixer, add the flour mixture, drained raisins and dates, and walnut pieces and mix by hand to obtain a soft, pliable dough.

In a small bowl, beat the remaining egg with the water. Separate the dough into 2 equal parts. On a lightly floured surface, roll each piece of dough into a 10 by 2-inch log. Flatten lightly and brush with the egg wash. Place the logs on the prepared baking sheet and bake until golden brown, 25 to 30 minutes. Transfer to a rack and let cool completely.

Decrease the oven temperature to 300°. Using a serrated knife, cut each log on the diagonal into ¼-inch-thick slices. Place them flat on the baking sheet. Bake until light gold on one side, 20 to 25 minutes. Turn them over and bake for 10 minutes longer. Let cool and store in a tightly sealed container for up to 2 weeks.

Bread Pudding with Candied Fruit

(Bezmat aux Fruits Confits)

Serves 6

read is considered sacred in Morocco. For this reason, no housewife would consider discarding even the smallest morsel. Remnants of stale, leftover bread, are toasted and crushed to make this dense, candied-fruit bezmat, *which is similar to a French* pain d'épices *(spice cake).*

¾ cup sugar
4 eggs, at room temperature
3 tablespoons sugar
¼ cup vegetable oil
1 cup unseasoned dried bread crumbs
1½ teaspoons baking powder
1 teaspoon ground ginger
1 teaspoon ground cinnamon
3 tablespoons mixed candied fruit, coarsely chopped
3 tablespoons raisins, plumped in warm water and drained

Preheat the oven to 375°. In a small saucepan over medium-high heat, cook ½ cup of the sugar, stirring continuously with a wooden spoon, until it turns a light amber and reaches the hard-crack stage (300° on a candy thermometer or turns hard when dropped into a saucer of cold water). This will take 8 to 10 minutes. Immediately pour the caramel into an 8 by 2-inch round nonstick cake pan. Tilt quickly to coat the bottom and the sides.

In a large bowl, using an electric mixer on medium speed, beat the eggs and remaining ¼ cup sugar until pale yellow. Slowly drizzle in the oil. With a spatula, fold in the bread crumbs, baking powder, ginger, and cinnamon. Add the candied fruit and the raisins. Pour the batter into the prepared mold.

Bake until a knife inserted in the center comes out clean, 35 to 40 minutes. Run a knife around the sides and immediately invert onto a serving platter (some of the caramel will remain in the pan). Serve warm or at room temperature.

My Mother's Russian Cake

(Le Russe de Ma Mère)

Serves 8

Connoisseurs who taste this seductive dessert of meringue and chocolate ganache will be reminded of a French dacquoise. Yet in Morocco this unforgettable flourless, butterless cake bears the intriguing name of Le Russe, *"the Russian." Look for superfine sugar in the baking section of supermarkets, or simply make it by grinding granulated sugar in a food processor.*

Meringue

6 egg whites, at room temperature
¼ teaspoon salt
¼ teaspoon cream of tartar
1¼ cups (10 ounces) superfine sugar

Ganache

1⅓ cups (7 ounces) hazelnuts, toasted and peeled (page 8)
3 tablespoons superfine sugar
7 ounces good-quality semisweet chocolate, broken into pieces
¼ cup brewed coffee (optional)
1 tablespoon brandy or rum
3 cups heavy whipping cream

Preheat the oven to 300°. Generously grease 3 (8¼-inch) pie pans or molds. Cut 3 rounds of waxed paper to line the bottom of each mold and generously grease the waxed paper.

To prepare the meringue, in a large bowl, using an electric mixer on high speed, beat the egg whites with the salt and cream of tartar. Slowly add the sugar and continue beating until stiff peaks form. Divide the egg whites among the three molds and smooth the tops with a spatula. Place in the oven and immediately decrease the heat to 275°. Bake until the meringue is hard but not brown, about 1 hour. (At this point, you can turn off the oven and let the meringues stand for a few hours or overnight.)

(continued)

To prepare the ganache, reserve 12 hazelnuts for garnish. In a food processor, grind the remaining nuts with 1 tablespoon of the sugar until you have a fine meal.

Combine the chocolate, coffee, brandy, and remaining 2 tablespoons sugar in a heatproof bowl. In a large, heavy skillet, bring water to a simmer over medium-high heat. Remove the skillet from the heat. Place the bowl filled with the chocolate mixture in the skillet and stir gently until the chocolate melts. Set aside and allow to cool slightly.

Pour the cream into a large chilled bowl and whip with an electric mixer on high speed until stiff peaks form. Gently fold the melted chocolate into the whipped cream, and then fold in half of the ground nuts.

To assemble the cake, carefully peel the paper from the bottom of each meringue. Set one round on a serving platter. With a spatula, spread one-third of the ganache over the top. Cover with a second round, and repeat the procedure. Top with the third round, and spread with the remaining ganache, spreading it over and around the sides of the cake. Sprinkle with the remaining ground hazelnuts and garnish with the whole nuts. Refrigerate for 2 to 6 hours before serving.

Pomegranate Seeds with Walnuts

(GRENADES AUX NOIX)

Serves 6

Since Biblical times, the pomegranate has symbolized fertility and abundance. The ancient Hebrews embroidered its image on the robes of their priests and used its likeness to decorate the pilasters of King Solomon's temple. Sephardic Jews feature the sacred fruit in this delicate, orange blossom–scented fruit salad served on the second evening of Rosh Hashanah.

4 pomegranates
3 tablespoons orange blossom water (page 6)
2 tablespoons sugar, or more
3 tablespoons water
⅓ cup walnut pieces, toasted (page 8)

To peel and seed the pomegranates, fill a large bowl with water. Cut the pomegranate in half vertically. Hold the fruit under water and break it apart, separating the seeds from the skin and the white pith. The seeds will sink and the pith will float to the surface. Transfer the seeds to a colander. Rinse and drain, removing any bits of skin and pith.

In a bowl, combine the pomegranate seeds, orange blossom water, sugar, and water. Cover and refrigerate for 2 to 3 hours. Taste and adjust the sugar if necessary. Add the walnuts just before serving. Serve in individual dessert bowls.

The Scent of Orange Blossoms

Dates Filled with Almond Paste

(Dattes Fourrées à la Pâte d'Amande)

Makes 2 dozen dates; serves 12

lmond paste confections and pastries occupy a prominent place on virtually every festive table. Homemade almond paste requires more work and patience, but is worth the effort. Some Sephardic cooks still employ a mortar and pestle to crush and pulverize their almonds instead of using a more modern food grinder.

1 cup whole blanched almonds
Zest of 1 large lemon, coarsely chopped
2 tablespoons water
6 tablespoons granulated sugar, plus additional for coating
1 tablespoon margarine
24 large pitted dates, slit open lengthwise

Preheat the oven to 250°. Place the almonds on a baking sheet and warm for 8 to 10 minutes. Remove from the oven and *slowly* feed them through a food grinder fitted with a coarse grinding plate. Switch to a fine grinding plate, and feed the almonds through 3 or 4 more times. Transfer to a bowl, add the zest, and mix thoroughly.

In a small, nonstick saucepan over medium heat, combine the water and sugar. Cook, stirring, until bubbles start to form, 2 to 2½ minutes. Immediately add the margarine and the almond-zest mixture. Stir continuously until the paste starts to pull away from the sides of the pan, 30 to 45 seconds. Transfer to a bowl to cool.

Spread some sugar on a plate. Mold a heaping teaspoon of the almond paste into a spindle shape and stuff inside a date. Compress the sides so the paste bulges out slightly. Roll in the sugar to coat. Using a knife, decoratively score the surface of the almond paste and set inside a 1-inch fluted paper cup. Continue in this manner until all the dates are filled. Serve immediately. Any leftover almond paste should be tightly wrapped with plastic wrap; it will keep for up to 3 months in the refrigerator. Return to room temperature before using.

Orange Blossom Jam

(Confiture de Fleurs d'Oranger)

Makes about 1½ cups

itter Seville oranges are best known as the variety with which the English produce their famous marmalade. In Morocco, Sephardic cooks use the tree's supremely fragrant blossoms to make this exotic jam. They carefully gather the flowers in the early morning from healthy, organic orchards.

12 ounces (6 cups) fresh pesticide-free orange blossoms
1 teaspoon salt
Sugar
½ cup water
3 tablespoons freshly squeezed lemon juice, strained
½ cup whole blanched almonds, toasted (page 8)

Gently pluck the petals off each blossom, discarding any that are blemished. In a large bowl, dissolve the salt and 2 tablespoons sugar in 3 cups water. Soak the petals for 30 minutes without handling them, then drain.

In a nonreactive saucepan, combine 4 cups water and 2 tablespoons sugar and bring to a boil. Add the petals and boil for 7 to 8 minutes. They should remain somewhat firm. Drain well. Using a scale, weigh the petals.

Weigh an equal amount of sugar (the amount should be approximately 6 ounces which would equal 1 cup). Place the weighed sugar in the saucepan along with an additional ½ cup sugar and the ½ cup water. (This will yield a thick syrup.) Gently swish the pan to blend the ingredients. Bring to a slow simmer over medium-low heat. Cook until the syrup thickens somewhat and the temperature registers 240° on a candy thermometer (a small amount of the mixture dropped into cold water will form a soft ball). Add the lemon juice and increase the heat to medium. Add the petals and stir gently with a wooden spoon. Cook, stirring occasionally, until the petals become translucent, 2 to 3 minutes. Remove from the heat. Let stand for 2 to 3 hours.

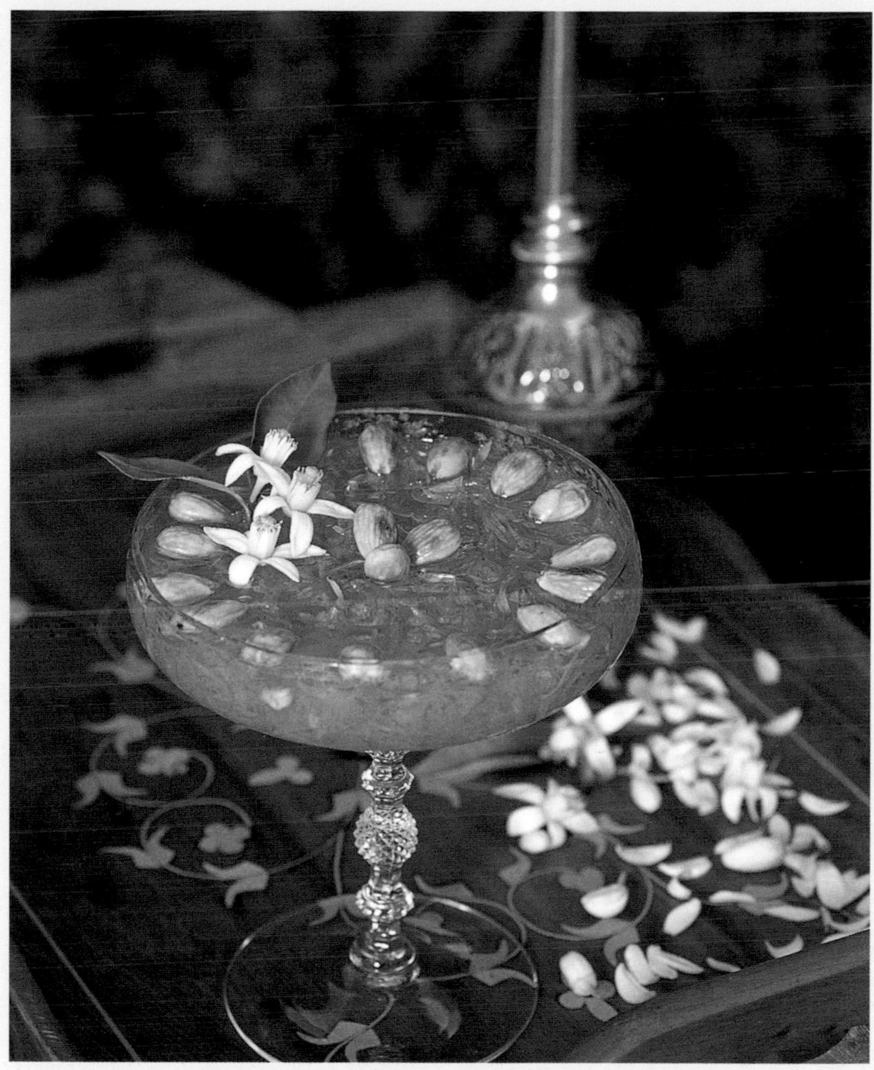

Bring the jam back to a slow simmer over medium-low heat. Cook until it turns a pale gold and the temperature once again registers 240° on the candy thermometer (a small amount of the jam dropped into cold water will form a soft ball). Remove from the heat and transfer to a sterilized jar. Allow to cool completely, seal, and refrigerate.

Spoon the jam into a small, shallow serving dish and surround with the almonds. Serve in individual saucers to savor with a small spoon.

Candied Oranges

(Oranges Confites)

Makes about 1 quart

itty's diminutive, nonagenarian great-grandmother was nicknamed "petit taxi" *for her dynamism in the kitchen. She was also queen of preserves. Decorative bowls of her delightful* oranges confites *appeared, as if by magic, within minutes of a guest's entry into her tidy Casablanca salon. Her great-grandchildren, as one might expect, were frequent and enthusiastic visitors.*

4 large unblemished oranges (about 2 pounds)
About 2 pounds granulated sugar
⅔ cup water
2 tablespoons freshly squeezed lemon juice, strained

Weigh the oranges. Weigh out an equal amount of sugar.

Using a fine grater, gently grate off and discard the zest of each orange. Place the fruit in a large bowl of water. Soak for 2 hours, then drain. In a large saucepan filled with boiling water, boil the oranges for 10 to 12 minutes. Drain and allow to cool. With a sharp knife, pierce each orange in four different places.

In a large nonreactive pot over low heat, combine the weighed sugar, water, and lemon juice, and cook, stirring occasionally, until no grittiness remains, 15 to 20 minutes. Do not let the mixture boil. Add the oranges and cook, turning them over every 5 minutes, for 30 minutes. Skim off the foam. Using a wooden spoon, gently press on the top of each orange to flatten it and let the syrup penetrate it. Continue cooking, turning the oranges every 15 minutes, gently pressing on the fruit until it acquires a translucent appearance, and the syrup turns a dark amber. This could take 1½ to 2 hours. Cooking time will vary depending upon the size of the oranges.

With a slotted spoon, transfer the oranges to a 2-quart glass jar. Pour the warm syrup into the jar through a fine-meshed sieve to remove any trace of foam. Seal and store at room temperature for up to 6 months. Present the oranges whole, then cut into wedges for serving.

The Scent of Orange Blossoms

Candied Grapefruit

(Pamplemousses Confits)

Makes about 2 quarts

ephardim enjoy nothing more than a saucer of ambrosial citrus preserves, chased with a demitasse of strong, black coffee. In the candying process, pink grapefruit turn dark amber in color; white grapefruit become golden.

3 large, unblemished white or pink grapefruit (about 3 pounds)
About 3 pounds sugar
¾ cup water
3 tablespoons freshly squeezed lemon juice, strained

Weigh the grapefruit. Weigh out an equal amount of sugar.

Using a vegetable peeler, remove and discard the thin layer of zest. With a fine grater, smooth the surface of the white pith. Place the fruit in a large bowl of water. Soak for 2 hours, then drain.

In a large saucepan filled with boiling water, boil the fruit for 10 to 12 minutes. Drain and repeat the process. Drain again and allow to cool. With a sharp knife, quarter the grapefruit. Carefully slice away and discard most of the pulp, leaving about ¼ inch of fruit along the rind.

In a large nonreactive pan over low heat, dissolve the weighed sugar, ¾ cup water, and lemon juice, stirring occasionally until all grittiness disappears, 15 to 20 minutes. Do not let the mixture boil. Add the rinds and cook, turning them over every 5 minutes, for 30 minutes. Skim off the foam. Using a sharp knife, pierce each rind in several places. Continue cooking, turning the rinds every 15 minutes, until they turn translucent and acquire a deep orange color and the syrup turns light amber. This could take up to 2 hours.

With a slotted spoon, transfer the rinds to a 2-quart glass jar. Pour the warm syrup into the jar through a fine-meshed sieve to remove any trace of foam. Seal and store at room temperature for up to 6 months. Serve the wedges of candied grapefruit in a decorative bowl.

Currant Preserves

(Mrouziya)

Serves 12

rouziya is one of the gastronomic highlights of the feast of La Mimouna. In times past, wealthy families hired a bevy of freelance cooks to assist in the painstaking process of seeding kilos of raisins. Today, most Sephardic cooks substitute seedless black currants instead.

1 pound dried black currants, rinsed quickly under running water
1¼ cups sugar
⅓ cup water, or more
Juice of ½ lemon
½ teaspoon ground cloves
15 walnut halves

In a large, nonreactive saucepan, combine the currants, sugar, and ⅓ cup water over medium heat. Cook, stirring occasionally, until the mixture begins to bubble gently, 8 to 10 minutes. Add the lemon juice and cloves. Decrease the heat to low and cook, stirring occasionally, until most of the water has evaporated. Add water, a tablespoon at a time, if the mixture becomes too dry. It should thicken and turn the color of dark caramel. This process may take 30 to 40 minutes.

Reserve 5 or 6 walnut halves for garnish. Combine the remaining nuts with the currant mixture and remove from the heat. Allow to cool and store in a tightly sealed container in the refrigerator.

Reheat the *mrouziya* over low heat for 20 to 30 minutes. Pour the warm preserve into a festive compotier, and garnish with the reserved walnut halves. Serve in individual saucers and savor with a small spoon.

Quince Compote

(Compote de Coings)

Serves 6

he exotic quince ripens in early fall, just in time for Rosh Hashanah. The aromatic fruit is a symbol of hope for all things "sweet" in the new year. This delectable compote graces every Sephardic table during the celebrations.

4 small quinces (about 2½ pounds)
1½ cups sugar
4 (3-inch) sticks cinnamon
1½ cups water

Peel and core the quinces and cut each into 8 wedges.

Place the quinces, sugar, and cinnamon in a nonreactive saucepan over medium-high heat. Add the water and bring to a boil. Cook, uncovered, until the fruit is fairly soft, 15 to 20 minutes. Decrease the heat to medium-low and continue to cook until the liquid attains the consistency of a light syrup, 30 to 35 minutes. Remove and discard the cinnamon sticks. Transfer the compote to a bowl and allow to cool. Serve at room temperature.

My darling daughters,

Cousin Guy arrives this afternoon from France. Knowing his weakness for mahiya apéritif, I have just returned from a mission to procure several bottles of the very best.

For outsiders, ferreting out a source for mahiya can be challenging. Cottage industries manufacturing the kosher eau-de-vie are considered almost clandestine operations. Distilleries shroud their location and techniques in secrecy. Names of artisans circulate in whispers, with reputations spread by word of mouth. I had to rely on the friend of a friend to introduce me to a woman reputed to make the finest mahiya in Fez. It is said she collects rainwater solely for the purpose of blending with the dry fruit prior to fermentation. Could this be her secret for producing mahiya of consistently high quality? Her fig mahiya is crystal clear with a hint of rosemary. The one she makes from cherries has a rich, reddish-brown hue. And her date mahiya seduces with a fragrance of wild fennel. I bought a small bottle of each for cousin Guy!

Besides serving it as an aperitif, your grandmother, like most other women of her generation, swore by mahiya's medicinal properties, from softening the discomfort of teething or colic to blunting a tenacious cough. You and your sister were the beneficiaries of its soothing effects on more than one occasion when you were girls.

Your loving mother

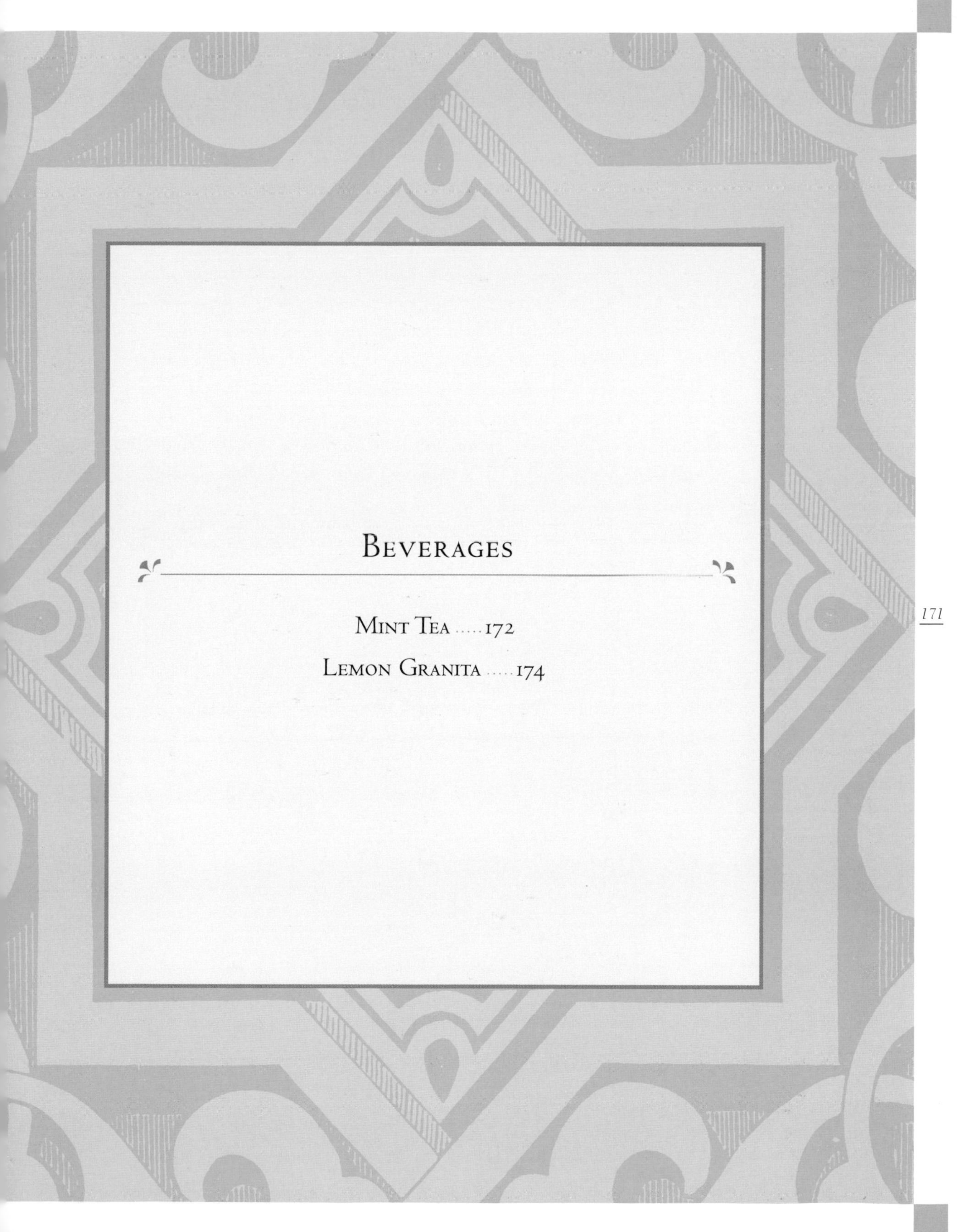

Beverages

Mint Tea 172

Lemon Granita 174

Mint Tea

(Atay b'Nahna)

Serves 6

int tea is the unofficial national drink of Morocco. In 1721, England's King George I sent several bales of tea as a gift to the court of Morocco's Sultan, Moulay Ismael. More widespread distribution did not begin until the naval blockade of the Crimean War in the 1850s, which forced the British to seek new markets. They found eager trading partners in the Jewish merchants of Essaouira. Mint tea can be enhanced with a few leaves of lemon verbena, or, when available, a few orange blossoms. Traditionally, one of two varieties of tea were used—Chinese gunpowder green and young hyson. Moroccans prefer their tea syrupy sweet and served in small, decorative glasses. We recommend adding sugar to taste.

1 tablespoon Chinese green tea
5 to 6 cups boiling water
30 to 40 fresh spearmint sprigs
½ cup granulated sugar

Rinse a teapot with boiling water. Discard the water and add the tea leaves to the pot. Add the boiling water and steep for 2 to 3 minutes. Add the mint and sugar to taste. Let stand for 3 to 4 minutes. Strain and serve immediately.

Hillula

Hillula is a day of pilgrimage. Believers gather annually at various shrines to participate in religious ceremonies honoring rabbinical holy men. Some shrines, like the one to Rabbi Amram Bendiouane in Ouezzane, attract both Jewish and Muslim followers. Pilgrims set lighted candles inside the trunk of an ancient olive tree, yet the tree miraculously never burns down. No special foods characterize a Hillula.

Picnic Lunch

Tomato Salad with Preserved Lemons (page 58)
Ground Meat Kebabs (page 109)
Lamb Kebabs (page 106)
Whole Wheat Rolls (page 68)
Fresh, seasonal fruit
Assorted pastries and Mint Tea (page 172)

Kitty's great-grandmother Dona (Maman) Darmon, Oran, Algeria, circa 1916.

Lemon Granita

(AGUA LIMÓN)

Serves 6

gua limón *is similar to Spanish* granizado *or Italian* granita. *Danielle recalls her addiction to a combination of* agua limón *and ice cream as a schoolgirl in Fez.* "C'était fameux!" *("It was fabulous!")* Agua limón *need not be frozen. Serve it simply, diluted with water, as an exotic lemonade.*

Zest of 7 lemons, grated
8 cups water
3 cups freshly squeezed lemon juice
1½ to 1¾ cups sugar
1 teaspoon vanilla extract
Mint leaves, for garnish

In a large bowl, combine the lemon zest with 4 cups of the water. Cover tightly with plastic wrap and refrigerate for 3 days. On the third day, strain the lemon water and discard the zest. Refrigerate. (The zest will absorb about ½ cup of the water.)

Strain the lemon juice several times through a very fine strainer. Combine with the remaining 4 cups water, sugar, vanilla, and lemon-infused water. Stir to blend. Taste and adjust the sugar, if necessary. Pour the liquid into a 9 by 13-inch metal baking dish. Freeze, uncovered, for 2 to 4 hours.

When the mixture is partially frozen, stir with a fork every 30 minutes, for about 2 hours, to maintain the consistency of a slush. Alternatively, freeze until hard. Ten minutes before serving, place the frozen mixture in a bowl and break it into chunks. Transfer to a blender or food processor, and pulse three or four times until you obtain the consistency of a slush.

Pour into tall glasses. Garnish with a mint leaf and serve with a spoon.

Sources

Caviar Assouline

Moroccan truffles and preserved lemons
505 Vine Street
Philadelphia, PA 19106
(800) 521-4491
www.assoulineandting.com

La Vigne Enterprises, Inc.

Preserved lemons
P.O. Box 2890
Fallbrook, CA 92088
(760) 723-9997
www.lavignefruits.com

Near East Foods

Orange blossom water, Moroccan truffles, and spices
4595 El Cajon Boulevard
San Diego, CA 92115
(619) 284-6361

Volubilis Imports

Moroccan kosher wines
P.O. Box 2393
La Jolla, CA 92038
(800) 865-8245
www.volubilis2000.com

Bibliography

Azuelos, Evelyne. *La Table Juive Marocaine*. Bègles: Editions Aviva, 1996.

Bloom, Carole. *The International Dictionary of Desserts, Pastries, and Confections*. New York: Hearst Books, 1995.

Chiche-Yana, Martine. *La Table Juive: Recettes et Traditions des Fêtes de l'Année Juive*. Tome 1. Aix-en-Provence: EDISUD, 1992.

Facciola, Stephen. *Cornucopia II, A Source Book of Edible Plants*. Vista, Calif.: Kampong Publications, 1999.

Gitlitz, David, and Linda K. Davidson. *A Drizzle of Honey: The Lives and Recipes of Spain's Secret Jews*. New York: St Martin's Press, 1999.

Hazan-Arama, Fortunée. *Les Saveurs de Mon Enfance: la Cuisine Juive du Maroc*. Paris: Editions Robert Lafont, 1987.

Le Tourneau, Roger. *Fès avant le Protectorat: Etude Economique et Sociale d'une Ville de l'Occident Musulman*. 2nd ed. Rabat: Editions Laporte, 1987.

Sternberg, Robert, Rabbi. *The Sephardic Kitchen: The Healthful Food and Rich Culture of the Mediterranean Jews*. New York: HarperCollins, 1996.

Tolédano, Joseph. *Les Juifs Maghrébins*. Belgique: Editions Brepols, 1989.

Voinot, Louis. *Causes Probables de la Commune Vénération: La Juiverie dans l'Antiquité*. Pélerinages Judéo Marocains. Paris: Larose, 1948.

Zafrani, Haim. *Mille Ans de Vie Juive au Maroc*. Paris: Maisonneuve-Larose, 1996.

Index

A

Abraham, 2, 24, 48, 49
Agua limón, 174
Ait Bouguemaz, xvi
Al Andalus, xvii, 28, 41, 90
Al Mahmun, 90
Almonds
  Almond and Walnut Macaroons, 142
  Couscous with Onion and Raisin Confit, 120–21
  Dates Filled with Almond Paste, 159
  paste, 4, 159
  Winter Squash with Caramelized Onions, 134
Aniseeds
  Aniseed Biscuits, 148–49
  toasting, 8
Antiochus IV Epiphanes, 104
Apikomenes, 49
Appetizers
  Chicken Phyllo Triangles, 35–37
  Holiday Potato and Meat Pie, 28–29
  Meat and Vegetable Frittata, 30–31
  Potato Pie, 32
Artichokes
  Meatballs with Swiss Chard, 95–96
  Pickled Vegetables, 16–17
Atay b'nahna, xvii, 172
Atlas Mountains, xv, xvi
Aubergines frites, 50
Azemmour, xvi, 102

B

Baraniya, xvii, xviii, 90–91
Beans. *See also* Fava beans; Garbanzo beans
  Dodie's Bean Soup with Preserved Lemons, 45
  Green Beans with Preserved Beef, 99
  soaking dried, 8
  Tangier-Style White Bean and Chard Soup, 41
Beef, fresh
  Beef Stock, 4
  Ground Meat Kebabs, 109
  Holiday Potato and Meat Pie, 28–29
  Meatballs in Cinnamon-Onion Sauce, 97
  Meatballs with Swiss Chard, 95–96
  Rosh Hashanah Cabbage Soup, 48
  Shabbat Stew, 113–16
  Tagine of Beef with Carrots and Turnips, 101
  Zahra's Beef with Preserved Kumquats, 102
Beef, preserved *(kleehe),* 98
  Green Beans with Preserved Beef, 99
  Potato Stew, 133
Beignets de hanoukka, 125
Bell peppers
  Danielle's Fresh Chile Hot Sauce, 13
  Danielle's Roasted Bell Peppers, 57

roasting, 7
Tita's Tomato and Bell Pepper Salad, 53
Bendiouane, Amram, 173
Berahoth, 2, 9
Berbers, xv, xvi
Beverages
Lemon Granita, 174
Mint Tea, 172
Bezmat aux fruits confits, 153
Biscotti, Date and Raisin, 150–51
Biscuits, Aniseed, 148–49
Biscuits au sésame, 146
Blettes aux citrons confits, 63
Boran, 90
Boundigaz aux blettes, 95–96
Boundigaz aux oignons, 97
Bouzaglou, David, 73
Bread
Braided Shabbat Loaf (Challa), 70–71
Bread Pudding with Candied Fruit, 153
Raisin Nut Bread, 76–77
Sephardic Pancakes, 78–79
Shabbat Sesame and Caraway Bread, 74–75
Whole Wheat Rolls, 68
Brochettes d'agneau, 106

C

Cabbage Soup, Rosh Hashanah, 48
Cakes
My Mother's Russian Cake, 154–56
Sponge Cakes, 145
Candied Carrots, 136
Candied Grapefruit, 165
Candied Oranges, 162
Carottes confites, 136
Carrots
Candied Carrots, 136
Pickled Vegetables, 16–17
Tagine of Beef with Carrots and Turnips, 101
Casablanca, 109, 162
Cassolita, 134
Challa, 70–71
Chard, 41
Chard Salad with Preserved Lemon, 63
Meatballs with Swiss Chard, 95–96
Tangier-Style White Bean and Chard Soup, 41
Chermoula, 132
Chicken
Chicken Fricassee, 88–89
Chicken Phyllo Triangles, 35–37
Chicken Stock, 5
Chicken with Garbanzo Beans, 84–85
Chicken with Onions and Tomatoes, 87
Meat and Vegetable Frittata, 30–31
Meatballs with Swiss Chard, 95–96
Roasted Chicken with Orange Juice, 83
Savory Wedding Flan, 138
Tagine of Chicken with Eggplant, 90–91

Chiles, 12
- Danielle's Fresh Chile Hot Sauce, 13
- Moroccan Hot Sauce (Harissa), 12

Chocolate
- My Mother's Russian Cake, 154–56

Citrons confits, 20
Compote de coings, 168
Condiment aux citrons confits, 21
Condiments
- Danielle's Fresh Chile Hot Sauce, 13
- Moroccan Hot Sauce (Harissa), 12
- Pickled Vegetables, 16–17
- Preserved Kumquats, 18
- Preserved Lemon Relish, 21
- Preserved Lemons, 20
- Salted Green Plums, 15

Confiture de fleurs d'oranger, 160–61
Cookies
- Almond and Walnut Macaroons, 142
- Date and Raisin Biscotti, 150–51
- Sesame Cookies, 146

Coquelets aux figues fraîches, 92
Cornish Hens with Fresh Figs, 92
Couscous, xvii, 5–6
- Couscous with Onion and Raisin Confit, 120–21
- Thursday Evening's Buttered Couscous, 124
- Turkey Couscous for Yom Kippur, 122–23

Couscous au beurre du jeudi soir, 124
Couscous à la dinde de Yom Kippur, 122–23
Couscous de la Mimouna, 120–21
Croquets, 150–51
Cucumber and Lemon Salad, 61
Currant Preserves, 166

D

Dafina, xvii, xviii, 112, 113
Dafina complète, 113–16
Danielle's Fresh Chile Hot Sauce, 13
Danielle's Roasted Bell Peppers, 57
Dates
- Date and Raisin Biscotti, 150–51
- Dates Filled with Almond Paste, 159

Dattes fourrées à la pâte d'amande, 159
Debdou, 86, 144
Desserts
- Almond and Walnut Macaroons, 142
- Aniseed Biscuits, 148–49
- Bread Pudding with Candied Fruit, 153
- Date and Raisin Biscotti, 150–51
- Dates Filled with Almond Paste, 159
- My Mother's Russian Cake, 154–56
- Pomegranate Seeds with Walnuts, 157
- Sesame Cookies, 146
- Sponge Cakes, 145

Deuteronomy, xvii–xviii
Diaspora, xv
Dietary laws, xvii–xviii
Dodie's Bean Soup with
  Preserved Lemons, 45
Dumplings, Fish, in Tomato
  Sauce, 128–29

E

Eggplant, 50
  Fried Eggplant, 50
  Tagine of Chicken with
    Eggplant, 90–91
Eggs
  Holiday Potato and Meat
    Pie, 28–29
  Meat and Vegetable Frittata,
    30–31
  Potato Pie, 32
  Savory Wedding Flan, 138
Egypt, departure from, 49
El Jadida, xvi
Epaule d'agneau rôtie, 105
Essaouira, xvi, 126, 172
Esther, Queen, 86

F

Fava beans
  Fresh Fava Bean Salad, 54
  Passover Fava Bean Soup, 42
  peeling, 7
Fennel
  Fresh Fennel Salad, 65
  Pickled Vegetables, 16–17
Feranne, 68, 102, 113
Fez
  dishes from, xv, 15, 35, 101,
    130, 131
  Hanukkah in, 125
  home life in, 44
  mellah in, xvi, xviii
  Rosh Hashanah in, 9, 48
  Yom Kippur in, 88
Figs, 137
  Cornish Hens with Fresh
    Figs, 92
  Figs in Orange Juice, 137
Figues au jus d'orange, 137
Fish
  Fish Dumplings in Tomato
    Sauce, 128–29
  Fish Fillets Fez Style, 130
  Fish Fillets with Garbanzo
    Beans, 131
  Fresh Sardine "Sandwiches,"
    126–27
Flan, Savory Wedding, 138
Fresh Fava Bean Salad, 54
Fresh Fennel Salad, 65
Fresh Sardine "Sandwiches,"
    126–27
Fricasada de pollo, 88–89
Fried Eggplant, 50
Frita, xviii
Frita de Tita, 53
Frittata, Meat and Vegetable, 30–31
Fruit, Candied, Bread Pudding
    with, 153

G

Galettes à l'anis, 148–49
Garbanzo beans
  Chicken with Garbanzo
    Beans, 84–85
  Fish Fillets with Garbanzo
    Beans, 131

Lentil and Garbanzo Bean Soup, 46–47
Shabbat Stew, 113–16
Sweet Roasted Vegetables for Rosh Hashanah, 117
Turkey Couscous for Yom Kippur, 122–23
Genesis, 137
George I, 172
Ginger, 87
Grapefruit, Candied, 165
Green Beans with Preserved Beef, 99
Grenades aux noix, 157
Ground Meat Kebabs, 109

H

Haketiya, xvi
Halla, 70
Hamman, 86
Hanukkah, 104, 125
Hanukkiyah, 104, 125
Haricots verts au kleehe, 99
Harira, 46
Harissa, 12
Harissa de Danielle, 13
Haroset, 49
Hazelnuts
My Mother's Russian Cake, 154–56
Hillula, 173
Holiday Potato and Meat Pie, 28–29
Holidays
Hanukkah, 104
Hillula, 173
Kappara, 24
La Mimouna, 62
Passover, 49
Purim, 86
Rosh Hashanah, 2–3
Shavuot, 72
Sukkoth, 33
Tisha B'Av, 144
Yom Kippur, 24

I

Ismael, Moulay, 172

J

Jam, Orange Blossom, 160–61
Jerusalem, xv, 104
Jnanat, xviii

K

Kappara, 24
Kashrut, xvii
Kebabs
Ground Meat Kebabs, 109
Lamb Kebabs, 106
Kefta, 109
Kessoua al kabira, 2, 34
Khbiza del zrarehe, 74–75
Khibats, 34
Kleehe, 98
Knidlats, 34
Kumquats, preserved, 18
Green Beans with Preserved Beef, 99
Zahra's Beef with Preserved Kumquats, 102
Kumquats au vinaigre, 18

L

La maguina, 30–31
Lamb
Lamb Kebabs, 106

Roasted Lamb Shoulder, 105
Tagine of Lamb with White Truffles, 111
Légumes sucrés de Rosh Hashanah, 117
Lemons, fresh
Cucumber and Lemon Salad, 61
Lemon Granita, 174
Pickled Vegetables, 16–17
Preserved Kumquats, 18
Lemons, preserved, 20
Chard Salad with Preserved Lemon, 63
Dodie's Bean Soup with Preserved Lemons, 45
Preserved Lemon Relish, 21
Tomato Salad with Preserved Lemons, 58
Lentil and Garbanzo Bean Soup, 46–47
Le Russe de ma mère, 154–56
Les poivrons de Danielle, 57
Letters, 9, 22, 34, 44, 73, 112, 125, 169
Leviticus, xvii
Loubia de Dodie, 45

M

Macaroons, Almond and Walnut, 142
Maccabeus, Judas, 104
Mafleta, 78–79
Maguina, 30–31
Mahiya, 44, 113, 169
Marrakech, xvi
Mauretania Tingitana, xv
Mazagan (El Jadida), xvi
Meat and Vegetable Frittata, 30–31
Meatballs
Meatballs in Cinnamon-Onion Sauce, 97
Meatballs with Swiss Chard, 95–96
Mellahs, xvi, 44, 102
Menus
Hanukkah, 104
Hillula, 173
La Mimouna, 62
Passover, 49
Purim, 86
Rosh Hashanah, 3
Shavuot, 72
Sukkoth, 33
Tisha B'Av, 144
Yom Kippur, 24
Mimouna, La, 62, 78, 120, 166
Mint Tea, xvii, 172
Mogador, xvi, xvii
Moroccan Hot Sauce (Harissa), 12
Moses, 72
Mount Sinai, 72
Mrouziya, 166
My Mother's Russian Cake, 154–56

N

Nuts. *See also individual nuts*
Raisin Nut Bread, 76–77
toasting, 8

O

Olive oil, 6
Olives, 6

Onions
- Chicken with Onions and Tomatoes, 87
- Couscous with Onion and Raisin Confit, 120–21
- Meatballs in Cinnamon-Onion Sauce, 97
- Winter Squash with Caramelized Onions, 134

Oran, Algeria, 40, 62, 72, 172

Orange blossoms
- Orange Blossom Jam, 160–61
- water, 6

Oranges
- Candied Oranges, 162
- Figs in Orange Juice, 137
- Roasted Chicken with Orange Juice, 83

Oranges confites, 162

Oriza aux patates douces de marisa, 119

Oriza of Wheat Berries and Sweet Potatoes, 119

Ouarka, 35

Ouezzane, 173

P

Pain aux raisins secs et aux noix, 76–77

Pallébés, 34, 145

Pamplemousses confits, 165

Pancakes, Sephardic, 78–79

Passover (Pesach), xv, xviii, 40, 42, 49, 54, 111. *See also* Mimouna, La

Passover Fava Bean Soup, 42

Pastela de pommes de terre, 32

Pastela des jours de fête, 28–29

Pastelitos de pollo, 35–37

Peppers. See Bell peppers; Chiles

Perry, Charles, 90

Pesach. *See* Passover

Petits pains complets, 68

Phoenicians, xv

Phyllo Triangles, Chicken, 35–37

Pickled Vegetables, 16–17

Pies
- Holiday Potato and Meat Pie, 28–29
- Potato Pie, 32

Plums, Salted Green, 15

Poisson à la Fassi, 130

Pollo con garbanzos, 84–85

Pomegranate Seeds with Walnuts, 157

Pommes de terre rôties à la chermoula, 132

Potaje Tangérois, 41

Potatoes
- Fish Fillets Fez Style, 130
- Holiday Potato and Meat Pie, 28–29
- Potato Pie, 32
- Potato Stew, 133
- Roasted Potatoes with Chermoula, 132
- Shabbat Stew, 113–16

Poulet aux oignons et aux tomates, 87

Poulet rôti au jus d'orange, 83

Preserves
- Candied Grapefruit, 165
- Candied Oranges, 162
- Currant Preserves, 166
- Orange Blossom Jam, 160–61
- Preserved Beef, 98

Preserved Kumquats, 18
Preserved Lemon Relish, 21
Preserved Lemons, 20
Quince Compote, 168
Prunes au sel, 15
Pudding, Bread, with Candied Fruit, 153
Purim, 76, 86

Q
Quenelles de poisson à la sauce tomate, 128–29
Quince Compote, 168

R
Raisins
Bread Pudding with Candied Fruit, 153
Couscous with Onion and Raisin Confit, 120–21
Date and Raisin Biscotti, 150–51
Raisin Nut Bread, 76–77
Winter Squash with Caramelized Onions, 134
Raiss, Abdelkrim, 73
Ramadan, 46
Ras el hanout, 23
Roasted Chicken with Orange Juice, 83
Roasted Lamb Shoulder, 105
Roasted Potatoes with Chermoula, 132
Rolls, Whole Wheat, 68
Rosh Hashanah, xv, xviii, 2–3, 9, 24, 48, 88, 117, 130, 146, 157, 168
Rosh Hashanah Cabbage Soup, 48

S
Saffron, 7–8
Salade de concombres et citrons, 61
Salade de fenouil cru, 65
Salade de févettes, 54
Salade de tomates aux citrons confits, 58
Salads
Chard Salad with Preserved Lemon, 63
Cucumber and Lemon Salad, 61
Fresh Fava Bean Salad, 54
Fresh Fennel Salad, 65
Tita's Tomato and Bell Pepper Salad, 53
Tomato Salad with Preserved Lemons, 58
Salé, xvi
Salted Green Plums, 15
Sardine "Sandwiches," Fresh, 126–27
Sardines mzouwejj, 126–27
Sausage
Dodie's Bean Soup with Preserved Lemons, 45
Shabbat Stew, 113–16
Savory Wedding Flan, 138
Seder, 40, 49, 111
Sefrou, 131
Sephardic Pancakes, 78–79
Sesame seeds
Sesame Cookies, 146
Shabbat Sesame and Caraway Bread, 74–75
toasting, 8
Shabbat, xvii, xviii, 32, 63, 70, 74, 97, 102, 112, 113, 124
Shabbat Sesame and Caraway Bread, 74–75

Shabbat Stew, 113–16
Shabel, 86
Shavuot, xviii, 72
Shofar, 2, 24, 48
Solomon, King, 157
Soupe au chou vert de Rosh Hashanah, 48
Soupe de fèves de Pessah, 42
Soups
    Dodie's Bean Soup with Preserved Lemons, 45
    Lentil and Garbanzo Bean Soup, 46–47
    Passover Fava Bean Soup, 42
    Rosh Hashanah Cabbage Soup, 48
    Tangier-Style White Bean and Chard Soup, 41
Spanish Inquisition, xv–xvi, 144
Spice blends
    chermoula, 132
    "Top of the Shop" Spice Blend, 23
Sponge Cakes, 145
Squash, Winter, with Caramelized Onions, 134
Stocks
    Beef Stock, 4
    Chicken Stock, 5
Sukkoth, xviii, 33, 84
Sweet Potatoes, Oriza of Wheat Berries and, 119
Sweet Roasted Vegetables for Rosh Hashanah, 117

T

Tagine d'agneau aux terfass, 111
Tagine de boeuf aux carottes et aux navets, 101
Tagines
    Cornish Hens with Fresh Figs, 92
    Tagine of Beef with Carrots and Turnips, 101
    Tagine of Chicken with Eggplant, 90–91
    Tagine of Lamb with White Truffles, 111
Talmud, xvii
Tangier, xvi, 41, 90, 133
Tangier-Style White Bean and Chard Soup, 41
Tea, Mint, xvii, 172
Tedouira, 46
Temrika, xvii, 112
Temrika de boeuf aux kumquats de Zahra, 102
Temrika del' hemms, 131
Temrika de patata, 133
Tétouan, xv, xvi, 84, 88, 134
T'faya, 138
Thursday Evening's Buttered Couscous, 124
Tisha B'Av, 144
Tita's Tomato and Bell Pepper Salad, 53
Tomatoes
    Chicken with Onions and Tomatoes, 87
    Fish Dumplings in Tomato Sauce, 128–29
    peeling and seeding, 7
    Tita's Tomato and Bell Pepper Salad, 53
    Tomato Salad with Preserved Lemons, 58
"Top of the Shop" Spice Blend, 23

Torah, 72
Truffes aux amandes et aux noix, 142
Truffles, White, Tagine of Lamb with, 111
Tu B'Shevat, 137
Turkey Couscous for Yom Kippur, 122–23
Turnips, Tagine of Beef with Carrots and, 101

V

Variantes, 16–17
Vegetables. *See also individual vegetables*
  Meat and Vegetable Frittata, 30–31
  Pickled Vegetables, 16–17
  Sweet Roasted Vegetables for Rosh Hashanah, 117
  Turkey Couscous for Yom Kippur, 122–23
Vinegar, 28
Visita, 34, 144, 145

W

Walnuts
  Almond and Walnut Macaroons, 142
  Pomegranate Seeds with Walnuts, 157
  Raisin Nut Bread, 76–77
  toasting, 8
Wedding Flan, Savory, 138
Wheat berries
  Oriza of Wheat Berries and Sweet Potatoes, 119
  Shabbat Stew, 113–16
Whole Wheat Rolls, 68
Winter Squash with Caramelized Onions, 134

Y, Z

Yom Kippur, xvii, xviii, 22, 24, 46, 88, 90, 122
Zahra's Beef with Preserved Kumquats, 102
Zeroua, 49